1,000,000 Books

are available to read at

www.ForgottenBooks.com

Read online
Download PDF
Purchase in print

ISBN 978-1-334-27753-5
PIBN 10601432

1 MONTH OF
FREE
READING

at
www.ForgottenBooks.com

By purchasing this book you are eligible for one month membership to ForgottenBooks.com, giving you unlimited access to our entire collection of over 1,000,000 titles via our web site and mobile apps.

To claim your free month visit:
www.forgottenbooks.com/free601432

English
Français
Deutsche
Italiano
Español
Português

www.forgottenbooks.com

Mythology Photography **Fiction**
Fishing Christianity **Art** Cooking
Essays Buddhism Freemasonry
Medicine **Biology** Music **Ancient
Egypt** Evolution Carpentry Physics
Dance Geology **Mathematics** Fitness
Shakespeare **Folklore** Yoga Marketing
Confidence Immortality Biographies
Poetry **Psychology** Witchcraft
Electronics Chemistry History **Law**
Accounting **Philosophy** Anthropology
Alchemy Drama Quantum Mechanics
Atheism Sexual Health **Ancient History**
Entrepreneurship Languages Sport
Paleontology Needlework Islam
Metaphysics Investment Archaeology
Parenting Statistics Criminology
Motivational

FRENCH
MARKET-GARDENING

INCLUDING

PRACTICAL DETAILS OF "INTENSIVE CULTIVATION" FOR ENGLISH GROWERS

BY JOHN WEATHERS

AUTHOR OF "A PRACTICAL GUIDE TO GARDEN PLANTS," ETC.

WITH A PREFACE BY WILLIAM ROBINSON

AUTHOR OF "THE ENGLISH FLOWER GARDEN," ETC.

WITH ILLUSTRATIONS

LONDON

JOHN MURRAY, ALBEMARLE STREET, W.

1909

PRINTED BY
HAZELL, WATSON AND VINEY, LD.,
LONDON AND AYLESBURY.

PREFACE

ALTHOUGH many kinds of fruits and flowers, and a few other crops like Cucumbers, Seakale, Tomatoes, Rhubarb, Mustard and Cress, have long been grown in British gardens on " intensive " principles, it is somewhat astonishing that the early production of other vegetables and salads has been left almost entirely in the hands of the French market-gardeners around Paris.

Just over forty years ago, Mr. Robinson was, I believe, the first to call the attention of the English-speaking world to the methods employed by the Parisian growers, who for generations past have practised the art of raising vegetables and salads to perfection during the worst months of the year. In the first edition of his admirable volume on *The Parks and Gardens of Paris*, he wrote : " We have several important things to learn from the French, and not the least among these is the winter and spring culture of salads—inasmuch as enormous quantities of these are sent from Paris to our markets during the spring months. . . . By the adoption of the French system salads may be grown to fully as great perfection near London and in the home counties as near Paris. The fact that we have to be supported by our neighbours with articles that could be so easily

v   *

produced in this country is almost ridiculous. It is
impossible to exaggerate the importance of this culture
for a nation of gardeners like the British ; and if it
were the only hint that we could take from the French
cultivators with advantage, it would be well worth
consideration."

Although this gospel was preached so long ago, but
little advance in the art of intensive gardening has
been made in the British Islands so far as vegetables
and salads are concerned. During the past year or
two, however, a keener interest has been awakened
on the subject. Not only has the horticultural press
devoted considerable attention to it, but the daily
papers have also discussed the matter. Among these
one especially, with characteristic enterprise, has
enthusiastically praised the system, and has almost
made one believe that it is quite a simple matter to
make a profit of £600 or £700 per annum out of an
acre of ground cultivated on the " French " system.

Perhaps a little too much emphasis has been laid
upon the profits to be derived from the system, and
there seems to be an impression amongst many who
possess no practical experience of gardening matters
whatever that fortunes are to be made easily by
growing Carrots, Cauliflowers, Lettuces, Radishes,
Turnips, etc., under lights or cloches. Many French
gardeners have no doubt reaped golden harvests as a
result of their industry, foresight, and skill ; but they
have been men saturated with all the details of their
profession gained entirely by experience.

There is no reason, however, why the British gardener endowed with similar energy, skill, and good
business capacity should not make the early production

of vegetables and salads a remunerative business, provided he is willing to do what his French neighbour does.

Many excellent gardeners are still under the impression that, although intensive cultivation may be all very well round Paris, it is not likely to be of great use in the British Islands. Even if this weak argument be used against the adoption of the system during the winter months, it cannot possibly be urged against its practice during the summer season. French and ˙English gardeners are then on a level footing. They both grow their salads in the open air without the aid of artificial heat. But what a difference is noticeable in the methods of cultivation, and in the amount of produce taken off a similar area of ground within a given period! On the English side of the Channel, Nature—with the help of an occasional hoeing, and a spasmodic or irregular watering—does most of the work on soil that has been treated in the ordinary way. Around Paris, however, not only is the soil made up of beautiful spongy mould from old and well-decayed manure, but water is given in such abundance during growth that Nature is encouraged to put forth all her energies in the shortest time. Added to this, there is the ingenious system of intercropping, by means of which the ground is covered with plants in all stages of growth, and one crop succeeds another as if by magic. During the summer months, at least, there is therefore little to prevent this system being carried out in Britain.

At the present time there is no book in the English language dealing with all the details of the French system of intensive cultivation as practised in the neighbourhood of Paris. Hence the appearance of this volume. The subject has been considered from a commercial gardener's point of view, the main object being to give reliable information on a subject that is now attracting great attention, not only throughout the British Isles, but in the United States and Canada. French gardens in England and around Paris have been visited, and the best French authorities on the subject have been consulted. Chief amongst these are the works of MM. Courtois-Gérard, Curé, and Potrat—all of which deal more or less exhaustively with the "culture maraîchère." I have also made frequent reference to Mr. Robinson's *Parks and Gardens of Paris*, and I am under still further obligation to the author of that work for the use of many of the woodcuts in this volume which he has generously placed at my disposal. In addition he has honoured me by writing an "Introduction" bearing directly upon a subject in which he has been personally interested for so many years. The other illustrations, apart from my own diagrams, have been kindly supplied by MM. Vilmorin, of Paris.

My best thanks are due to Mr. George Schneider, President of the French Horticultural Society in London; to MM. Aquatias and Lecoq, formerly of Mayland; and to M. Adolphe Beck, the pioneer of French gardeners in England, for the information they so readily gave me on many points.

In regard to the names of the different varieties of vegetables and salads mentioned in this work, the French names as well as the recognised English names have been given in most cases, in the hope that it may prove a convenience.

JOHN WEATHERS.

CONTENTS

PART I

GENERAL

PART II

SPECIAL CULTURES

CONTENTS

PART III

LIST OF ILLUSTRATIONS

INTRODUCTION

THERE is no contrast in the farm or garden world more striking than that between the market-gardens of London and Paris : about London broad sweeps in the Thames valley, wind-swept, shelterless, well farmed ; about Paris close gardens, walled in, richly cultivated, and verdant with crops, even at the most inclement time of the year, and with not an inch of space wasted with paths. And this is not owing to the differences of climate, although people say, whenever one speaks of it, " It is a question of climate." I do not know a worse climate in winter than that of Paris, the season when the gardeners get their most profitable results. For all green things our climate is, if anything, a shade better than theirs. The very fact of the little cloche covering acres proves that the climate of Paris is not so good. The late M. Henri de Vilmorin used to tell me that his father had much considered the market-gardens of the two capitals, and estimated that the French grower of vegetables got at least four times the quantity obtained in the larger and broader cultures round London. Be it noted here that this book concerns the limited culture of the Paris market-gardens, for around Paris, as around London, there is the large field culture of vegetables. There is good soil round Paris in the Seine valley, and we cannot complain of the soil in the valley of the Thames—it is a totally different system and plan we have to look to.

The cloche is a great worker for the grower, and defies a harsh climate, as, combined with good soil and culture, it enables the French gardener to supply so many of the markets of Britain and Western Europe with salads and other early and welcome things. The use and work of the cloche well deserve study on the part of gardeners. The packing and moving of cloches require much care, if we are not to lose the half of them, and we should not want makers of them over here. Surely our own glass people should be able to supply us. It was one trouble of the imported cloches that if not very carefully packed half of them were lost on the way. Even without the finely prepared soil of the Paris gardens, they are most useful in various other ways, and I strike my Tea Roses under them in the autumn, and get the early tender green things in the spring. They are also an excellent aid in propagation.

It should be borne in mind that the soil of the French market-garden is not really a soil as we understand it, but very often is almost decayed manure—old hot-beds, in fact—that, mixed with a good natural soil below, makes the conditions of soil about as good as they can be.

The French cook is a great aid, because, master in his domain, he insists on having things of the right quality and right age. In the Paris market you never see the coarse razor-bill beans of our market, nor carrots scarcely fit to offer to a horse, because over all vegetables the cook exercises control. If our English cooks were to have the same power it might help to put a stop to the practice of sending coarse vegetables to our markets. Once, speaking to a leading grower of peaches at Montreuil, I asked his opinion of certain new peaches more remarkable for size than for good flavour, and he said,

" If we were to send in those peaches to our customers they would be promptly sent back to us " !

The clever way of intercropping in these gardens is instructive, and might be carried out almost anywhere. Weeks before a given crop is ready for cutting another crop, usually of a different nature, is planted between, and when the first crop is cut the new one is ready to spread itself out and occupy the whole of the ground. The partial shade of the first crop does the young plants no harm. This is one way of getting a good deal off the ground. This plan is carried out to some extent by cottage gardeners in England, who are often good gardeners.

This book is the work of a thoroughly trained gardener (a better word than horticulturist) ; it is sure to be helpful to all those who are interested in this question, and goes as far as a book can. I think in all these interesting cultures we ought to do a little more than book or college work. We should send young men abroad after due training, the farmer to Germany and Hungary, the gardener to France. There is so much more to be learnt by actual contact with soil, climate, surroundings—everything. They speak to us in a way that no book ever can. And the same thing may be said in regard to forestry and nursery work ; but the men who are to do this kind of work should be well-trained men—that is, men who have been trained in several good gardens, so that they might be able to judge of the value of what they saw.

Those who think of attempting such gardening in our country should remember that this very special culture is for the most valuable crops, and that the work is done in the best conditions by unremitting labour of trained men. In France, as in our own country, for ordinary things there is the open field culture. Also there are in France and in all countries certain things that have to be grown in the best natural conditions and soils if their finest qualities are to be secured—such things as asparagus, for example, and even the wild-flavoured turnips we see in our markets in spring; and whether we deal with plants, or horses, or cattle, or sheep, no skill can take the place of the natural conditions that suit them best.

For the special cultures round Paris a good supply of water is essential, and this cannot be commanded so well in open field culture. In the British Islands the supply of water is so copious that, except in the south and east, we seldom feel the want of it; but in the London district, in hot summers, the markets sometimes suffer, and therefore a good water supply in all parts of the choice garden is a gain. I noticed in the Chinese gardens in California a striking resemblance to French ways in their thorough culture, absolute cleanliness, and immediate supplies of water; and everything suggested some old-world connection between the two.

W. ROBINSON.

FRENCH MARKET-GARDENING

PART I

GENERAL

THE MEANING OF "INTENSIVE" CULTIVATION

THE term "intensive" cultivation is now used to indicate the particular methods employed by market-gardeners or "maraîchers" in the neighbourhood of Paris to produce early crops of salads and vege-tables at a season of the year when they are most likely to realise high prices in the market. These early crops are known as "primeurs" amongst French gardeners; and to secure them at just the right moment necessitates intimate knowledge as to the soil, temperature, and general treatment re-quired by each particular crop to bring it to perfection. Intensive cultivation differs from the ordinary methods of culture, inasmuch as it means, in addition to know-ledge, incessant care and attention. Comparatively small areas of ground are used by growers, and it may be said that at no time during the year is the land free from crops of one kind or another. Indeed, several crops are grown on the same patch of land simultaneously, as mentioned further on in the pages of this work. The great aim seems to be to grow together crops of quite different natures, so that the growth of one shall not interfere with the proper development of the other before it is gathered.

"The culture of salads for the Paris market," said Mr. Robinson forty years ago in his *Parks and Gardens of Paris*, "is not merely good—it is perfection." The same opinion holds good to-day, and there can be no doubt that in many parts of the British Islands, where the climate is kinder to the gardener than in the neighbourhood of Paris, it is within the region of possibility to grow produce that would rival if not surpass what is imported from abroad.

Although much attention has been directed to the French methods of growing such early crops as Carrots, Radishes, Cauliflowers, Turnips, Lettuces, etc., there are at present few establishments in England where the system is practised on *bona-fide* commercial lines. The first garden of the kind was established at Evesham in the year 1905, but it soon passed from the hands of the original owner. What may be called an experimental and educational garden on intensive cultivation has also been established at Mayland, in Essex, by Mr. Joseph Fels. No expense has been spared in fitting up this garden with all modern appliances, and a capital outlay of some £2,000 to £3,000 has been incurred. The ordinary market-gardener, however, no matter how intelligent or skilful he may be, is not likely to look upon such a large initial outlay with great favour, knowing as he does from practical experience the fluctuations of the markets, and the fickleness of the public taste.

While it may not be necessary to spend anything like £2,000 or £3,000 when starting a French garden, it is simply preposterous to imagine—as some do—that the intensive system of cultivation can be adopted on remunerative lines without incurring some expense. Cloches, frames, manure, and water—the four great feet of the system—must be provided before a start can be made, and what these are likely to cost may be seen from the figures given at p. 25.

Besides the French gardens at Evesham and in Essex, there are others, such as the one at the Burhill Golf Club, Walton, and the notable one at Thatcham in Berkshire. This garden has been much boomed in the daily press, and is undoubtedly a most interesting object-lesson as to what can be done by women. It is managed entirely by ladies, with the help of a French gardener or " maraîcher " ; and I should say that it was established on reasonable and economic lines. The garden occupies about 2 acres, and is on a fairly rich sandy loam, with a gentle slope to the south. The land has been fenced in all round, and notwithstanding the fact that most of the manure has to be carted from Reading, a distance of 14 miles, and works out at 7s. per ton, I was informed that very good results were obtained. Water is obtained from a well that has been sunk 40 feet deep, but it is to be made deeper. Last year the storage tank held only 500 gallons of water ; this was found to be much too small, and it was necessary to keep the oil engine pumping all day to secure a sufficient supply.

That profits are to be made out of French gardening there can be no doubt, and an attempt has been made at p. 26 to show what they are likely to be. The figures given may be considerably below the mark so far as profits are concerned, and if so, so much the better. It is always as difficult to estimate profits in advance as it is to count chickens before they are hatched. In any case, profits depend upon so many factors—the personality of the grower, his skilfulness as a cultivator, his knowledge of the markets, his business ability, etc.—any one of which neglected or overlooked at a critical moment may easily upset the best-laid schemes, and end in loss instead of profit.

There is one thing about commercial gardening from which we cannot get away, and that is—expenses *must* be incurred if any profit at all is to be made.

HISTORY OF INTENSIVE CULTIVATION IN FRANCE

Some people are inclined to think that the present system of intensive cultivation as practised in the market-gardens (or " marais," as they are called) in the neighbourhood of Paris is an old English system that was dropped years ago and is now being revived. I do not think it is anything of the kind. The English gardener has had his system all along, and the French gardener his—each sticking more or less obstinately to his own.

The system described in this work is by no means new, but I think it may be looked upon as being almost exclusively French, if not entirely Parisian. Claude Mollet, the first gardener to Louis XIII. of France (*b.* 1601, *d.* 1643), seems to have been the first great exponent of it, judging from his *Théâtre du Jardinage*, published in 1700. Another French gardener, La Quintinye (*b.* 1626, *d.* 1688), whose *Instruction pour les Jardins fruitiers et potagers* was published in 1690, also deals with the subject and tells how he was able to send to the table of Louis XIV., surnamed " the Great " (*b.* 1638, *d.* 1715), Asparagus and Sorrel in December ; Radishes, Lettuces, and Mushrooms in January ; Cauliflowers in March ; Strawberries early in April ; Peas in May ; and Melons in June.

From this it may be gathered that the art of intensive cultivation even in the seventeenth century was by no means in its infancy. Frames were already in use, and long before them cloches were common.

From the time of Louis XIII. to that of Louis XVIII. —that is, from about the year 1600 to 1800—great progress seems to have been made ; and garden after garden was established in Paris and its environs. The troubles of the Revolution and the wars of the Empire, however, interfered a good deal with the development of the system for the time being. But in 1844, according to Courtois-Gérard, about 1,500 acres of land were devoted to intensive cultivation in Paris. This area was in the hands of 1,125 growers, so that each had an average of not much more than an acre.

Since that time great alterations have taken place owing to the construction of railways, new boulevards, and other improvements, the result being that many of the old Parisian market-gardens have completely vanished. On the outskirts of Paris, however, several hundreds of gardens have been established, and it is computed that about 1,300 growers practise the intensive system of cultivation at the present time on about 3,000 acres of land. These growers have about 460,000 lights, and from 5,000,000 to 6,000,000 bell-glasses or cloches among them. The largest number of lights used by a single individual is said to be 1,400, and the smallest 60 ; while the greatest number of cloches used by one man is said to be 5,000, the lowest number being 100.

The produce grown by these market-gardeners is considered to be worth over half a million sterling yearly—giving an average of about £400 to each grower.

WORK IN A FRENCH GARDEN

Those who produce early vegetables and salads have by no means an easy time in French gardens proper. Every one is awake before daylight, and the women play their part as well as the men. In summer they are often up at 2 o'clock in the morning, and in winter at 4 o'clock, so as to be ready to sell the produce at the central markets. When they return home they attend to such work as weeding, and packing, or pulling the vegetables for the following day's market. In all their work they are assisted by their daughters, and although the work is not exactly rough, it is nevertheless very tiring, because they are often obliged to kneel on the ground for the greater part of the day regardless of the season or the weather.

The men commence work after the women have gone to market. At 7 o'clock in the morning they munch a crust whilst at work, and at 9 o'clock all go to breakfast. In the summer time, owing to the heat, they rest for one or two hours at mid-day and all have dinner together like a family. After dinner, each one works on again without interruption until supper time, which takes place at 10 o'clock in summer and at 8 o'clock in winter. During the evening the men water the crops, make mats, carry leaf-soil, manure, etc. At the same time the women arrange the produce in baskets, crates, or hampers according to requirements, after which the waggon is loaded so that everything shall be in readiness for the market. Such is the picture of a French maraîcher's or market-gardener's life as drawn by Courtois-Gérard in 1844, and it is apparently much the same now. Certainly, one has only to pay a visit to the Halles Centrales—as the Paris markets are called—to see at a glance what an important part the wives and daughters of the French market-gardeners play in the great industry we are considering. Are those who wish to make fortunes out of the land in the British Islands willing to work like French men and French women ? That is the point.

THE SITE FOR A FRENCH GARDEN

When choosing a site for a French garden it is essential to select a piece of land quite free from trees and shrubs, and away from high buildings that cast a shade. The ground should be either flat or with a gentle slope in any direction between the south-east and south-west ; and if rectangular in shape, so much the better. A position too close to the sea-coast should be avoided, especially in very windy localities, as the briny spray from the ocean will do much damage to tender vegetation.

Protection from the cold winds from the north and east, and also against south-westerly gales, is more or less essential—in the latter case chiefly on account of the damage that is likely to be done to lights and cloches. Good walls, close wooden fences, or thick hedges should be erected for the purpose. Walls and fences may be utilised for growing various kinds of fruit-trees, but in the French gardens I visited I noticed that the walls all round were quite bare, and were merely shelters. One grower, indeed, informed me that it was scarcely worth while trying to grow fruit-trees on the walls, as they would be more trouble than they were worth.

Personally, however, I should imagine that good kinds of fruit-trees trained on a wooden fence or wall would not interfere with the culture of vegetables and salads, and would be a source of income in due course.

BORDERS.—In every " French " garden it is usual to have a border from 6 to 12 ft. wide round the walls or fences, such borders being often raised at the back and sloping towards the front, especially when having a south aspect. According to the season, various vegetables are grown on these borders. For example Cos Lettuces raised under lights or cloches may be planted out on a south border in January, or early in February, after a sowing of Radishes and Early Carrots has been previously made on the same soil ; and Cauliflowers raised in autumn and protected in frames during the winter may be planted between the Lettuces in March. These various crops will mature at different times— the Radishes, Lettuces, and Carrots being gathered long before the Cauliflowers ; and when the last-named have matured the border may be utilised for Cucumbers, Endive, Lettuce, Spinach, etc., according to requirements.

On the borders facing east and west similar crops may be sown or planted. The aspect, however, not being so genial as that facing south, crops mature somewhat later.

The north border also has its uses. In summer it may be used for raising Spinach, Turnips, Lettuce, etc., which enjoy a little shade during the great heat of summer. Or such an aspect may be used for storing the idle frames during the summer, or for building a shed in which lights, mats, etc., not in use may be packed away.

I have seen the frames packed up on each other a dozen or more high so as to be out of the way of crops. The cloches are also stacked up close together in heaps of four and five (as shown in fig. 6), and even during the summer months when not in use are covered with old mats or straw. This is to protect them from the hail-storms which sometimes suddenly come on with great violence in Paris. Indeed, in August 1908 I saw a Vitry garden where sad havoc had been made amongst the cloches during a hail-storm in July.

In a " French " garden protection is of such vital importance that where neither walls nor hedges exist, it is essential to erect a fence of some sort as a guard against the wind.

THE SOIL AND ITS TREATMENT

Although so much manure is used in the process of intensive cultivation, one must, nevertheless, not overlook the fact that a good natural soil in the garden is of the utmost importance. The seeds of many crops may be sown in the open air, from which the plants will later on be transferrred to frames or cloches. And again, plants raised in frames may be transplanted to the open ground according to circumstances. If the soil, therefore, is already in good condition it will mean not only good growth of the crops but also a great saving in labour and manures. An ideal garden soil for ordinary purposes should consist of about 40 parts clay, 35 parts sand, 10 parts lime, and 15 parts humus, in every hundred. With proper digging, or occasional trenching, and a fair supply of manure—say about 16 tons to the acre—such a soil will yield excellent results, especially in genial and sheltered localities. Indeed, for vegetables and salads I think much more manure than this might be used in a well-rotted state than is at present usual in ordinary gardens : 20 to 30 tons to the acre would not be too much.

Where wet, cold, and heavy clay exists, it will require modifying with the addition of sand or grit, and humus, in addition to deep cultivation. If, on the other hand, the soil is light and sandy or gravelly, it will be improved by the addition of heavy loam, chalk, or marl, as well as plenty of manure—especially from the cowshed or piggery.

Where, however, frames and cloches are used extensively for early crops grown on hot-beds, the soil beneath is not of such vital importance, as the roots of the plants do not touch it. I remember that the soil in the " French " garden at Mayland, Essex, was little better than harsh brick earth, and yet some magnificent crops were produced in the frames and cloches upon the beds and composts that had been specially prepared for them.

Whatever the soil may be, it is essential to have it cleared of weeds and rubbish prior to digging and levelling, so that it will be a fairly easy matter to mark out the lines where the frames and beds are to be laid down.

PLANNING OUT THE GROUND.—Having decided upon the number of frames to be used and hot-beds to be made it is necessary to mark the ground out in parallelograms with a narrow pathway or alley between each. The frames used by the French growers are 4 ft. 5 in. in width. Consequently, the beds will be made wide enough to take them. As the ground in Paris is exceedingly dear—often £30 or £40 per acre—the French growers cannot afford to waste any space. Hence the alley or pathway between one range of frames and another is reduced to the least possible width. This is generally about 12 in.—but often only 9 in.—just sufficient to allow a man to walk between them carefully. In places where land is not excessively dear, it is scarcely necessary to have such narrow pathways, as they are by no means easy for the novice to negotiate. One must, however, remember that the wider pathways will absorb much more manure for banking up or " lining " the frames in winter than the narrow ones ; consequently, wide pathways would be a source of considerable expense.

PREPARING THE BEDS.—Having marked out the ground, the soil in the beds is then broken up with the fork. The rake is afterwards passed over it to make level, and any clods or stones are drawn into the pathways. Here they are left to be trodden down, because it is generally an advantage to have the pathways somewhat higher than the surface of the beds. If the beds are higher than the pathways the water runs off the beds away from the roots of the plants, so that the latter are likely to suffer.

The beds should run as near as possible east and west, so that the frames shall slope towards the south. If this position cannot be secured the next best is between the north-west and south-east, the object in both cases being to secure as much light and heat as possible from the sun for the plants beneath the lights.

SLOPING BORDERS.—It often happens that borders cannot be made in sheltered places against walls, hedges, or fences, and they are then made in the open.

A piece of ground is marked out about 6½ ft. wide and is deeply dug all over. On the south side a trench about 2 ft. 3 in. is then made about 6 in. deep, and the soil from it is placed on the northern edge of the remaining piece of soil. This is about 4 ft. 3 in. wide, so as to accommodate three rows of cloches when " angled " with each other. The back of the bed, *i.e.* the northern side, is made firm by patting with the spade, and is kept straight with the aid of a line tightly stretched from one end to another. The trench forms the pathway, and the soil from it serves to raise the bed so as to make the surface incline towards the south. The surface is levelled with the rake, and it will be noticed from the sketch (fig. I) that the cloches in the first row are almost on the level, while the two behind are raised up. If the soil at the back drops down into a slope,

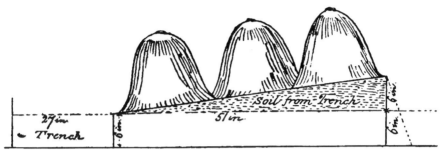

FIG. I.—RAISED SLOPING BED FOR CLOCHES.

it may be chopped down straight with the spade, and spread over the surface ; or it may be left to buttress up the entire bed.

WATER SUPPLY

Without a good supply of water the cultivation of early produce on the French system is out of the question. One of the most important points, therefore, to bear in mind when selecting a site for a French garden is to find out whether there is likely to be an abundance of water or not. In the great majority of cases it may be impossible or ruinously expensive to have water from any of the companies. It must, therefore, be secured either from streams, ponds, or wells. In any case, it will be necessary to secure it in such large quantities that the supply is not likely to fail at a critical moment.

In a garden of any size, remote from companies' water mains, it will be necessary to have a large storage tank erected at a height of about 20 feet. To get the water into the tank from a stream or a well, various kinds of pumps are used. Windmills, gas, oil, or electric pumps, " rams," and pulsometers are in use, and are all more or less useful for throwing large quantities of water. Windmills are favoured by many growers. They have, however, the drawback—so far as intensive cultivation is concerned—of lying " becalmed " on a broiling hot summer's day when there is not enough wind to stir a leaf, and perhaps just when the crops are in the greatest need of water. Assuming that water is available in sufficient abundance, perhaps a pump driven by a gas, oil, or electric engine is on the whole most reliable. I have seen them all at work, and consider where electric current can be obtained at a cheap rate from adjacent mains that the electric pump requires the least outlay of capital, and requires the minimum of attention. I saw such an electric pump at work in the outskirts of Paris, and the starting and stopping was simplicity itself—merely pushing a small lever over a distance of an inch or two.

Although windmills and gas, oil, or electric pumps will throw large quantities of water, they all suffer from one drawback in common—namely, that the water obtained is almost, if not quite, ice-cold in winter. The application of ice-cold water to tender crops growing in a temperature of from 65° to 75° Fahr. would be probably fatal to the plants. If not, it would at least cause stagnation of growth, and induce chills and other troubles. For this reason one is almost inclined to favour the " pulsometer " as a suitable pumping-machine, simply because it takes the chill off the coldest water, and in winter-time the plants and soil may be moistened with water of a genial tepidity. The great drawback, however, to a " pulsometer " seems to be that it will not pump until steam has been " got up " in the necessary boiler attached. It also requires the almost constant attendance of a man to keep the fire well fed with coke or coal ; and this last item is likewise a source of considerable expense.

With any of the other pumps mentioned, the difficulty of heating the water in the storage tank may be got over fairly easily. By fixing up a small, ordinary " saddle " boiler, and connecting it to the storage tank with a " flow " and " return " pipe, sufficient heat will be generated with a barrow-load or two of coke per day ; so that the temperature of the water is easily raised to the region of 60° to 70° Fahr., or even more if the boiler is " driven."

As little or no water is actually applied overhead directly to the plants growing on the hot-beds and under cloches during the coldest period of the year, say from November or December till March or April, the question of heating the water in the storage tanks in winter is not of paramount importance perhaps, unless the liquid is required for use in hot-houses and greenhouses.

CAPILLARY ATTRACTION.—During the cold winter season, the early crops in the frames derive all the moisture they require at the roots from the rainwater that runs off the lights on to the rather long, littery manure in the narrow pathways between the hot-beds. By capillary attraction the water is absorbed from the sodden pathways to the centre of the beds beneath the lights, and in this way the tender plants secure it after the chill has been taken off by the warm manure. The application of water in this indirect way also accounts for the narrowness of the hot-beds used, as it is obvious that in the case of wide beds it would be impossible for the water to reach the centres by means of capillary attraction alone.

The crops under cloches, of course, secure moisture in the same way, only more easily.

DISTRIBUTION OF THE WATER.—To secure a proper distribution of water over the garden it is advisable to have pipes laid on from the storage tank or a company's main. The pipes should be 3 or 4 in. in diameter to secure a good and easy flow of water in all directions. If the tank is also placed sufficiently high—say, 20 to 25 feet—there will be good pressure of water, so that when a hose-pipe is attached to any of the stand pipes—placed at regular and convenient intervals—it will be possible to water the contents of several frames without inconvenience.

In addition to the hose-pipes, it is also advisable during the summer months to have several galvanised tanks, or even barrels, placed where they are most likely to be useful when Melons are being watered by waterpots. Indeed, the more conveniently a garden and its appliances are arranged the better, more comfortable, and the more economic will the working be on the whole. A slip-shod or ill-digested scheme of arrangement is likely to lead to endless troubles afterwards, when it may be difficult to rectify defects without considerable expense.

MANURES

In addition to a plentiful supply of water there must also be a bounteous, almost a prodigious, quantity of manure available—and the best stable manure into the bargain ; otherwise intensive cultivation is quite out of the question. Good stable manure costs anything from 4s. to 7s. per ton ; and 1,000 tons annually may be required for a garden of two acres. The first year, naturally, is more expensive in every way than succeeding years, and with the progress of time somewhat smaller quantities of manure may suffice.

When the manure becomes old or spent it is not useless. It gradually becomes trodden down into fine black particles, and in this condition of vegetable mould is a most important ingredient in the soil of every French garden. In some old Parisian gardens I visited, the manure of former years covered the original soil to a depth of two or three feet, and it almost felt as if one was walking on a velvet pile carpet. This old manure, decayed into fine particles, assumes a deeper and deeper tint with age, and yields up its fertilising foods under the influence of air, water, and heat for the benefit of the crops grown upon it. It is used over and over again for spreading over the open borders, over the hot manure in the frames, and over the cloche beds, in layers of varying thickness, and the tender rootlets have no trouble whatever in penetrating its moist, warm, and spongy tissues.

Besides good stable manure, other manures—such as that from cows, pigs, sheep, etc.—are also freely used by some growers, as well as night soil when ob-

2

tainable, and when no strong objections are raised on the question of odour. Many French housewives, with characteristic thrift, never waste any refuse from the house, the poultry run, or the kitchen garden, if it is likely to be at all useful in the culture of vegetables or salads. In fact, anything in the shape of animal or vegetable refuse is carefully preserved, and made into a compost heap mixed with leaves, weeds, and soil. It is then freely and frequently drenched with soapy water on washing days as well as with any other household liquids available. In due course this organic refuse (which is taken away by the dustman in England) becomes converted into a beautiful rich and friable mould.

Chemical or *artificial manures*, although now so extensively employed in ordinary gardening practice, are not popular with intensive cultivators. And it is questionable, even in the event of stable manure becoming scarcer owing to the more general adoption of motor-cars, if chemical manures would ever produce the same excellent results that are now secured from hot-beds with their equable and genial warmth.

The use of hot-water pipes scarcely requires consideration for somewhat similar reasons. They dry and bake and parch the soil so regularly, that the tender roots of crops would soon be shrivelled up unless the lights were frequently taken off to drench the beds with water: and this is a dangerous proceeding during the winter months, and likely to result in total loss of the crops.

TREATMENT OF A MANURE HEAP.—So as to avoid waste and secure the best results, it is necessary to manage a manure heap with a certain amount of care and intelligence. During the summer months hot manure is not required, but large quantities are secured and are kept in reserve until autumn, when the beds are made. On the outskirts of Paris enormous heaps of manure may be seen during the summer months, and in August men may be seen with bare legs and trousers turned up to the knees, turning over the heaps and watering them copiously. The straw or litter is forked out and kept in conical heaps by itself. The short and more or less well-rotted portion which is left should also be made into similar conical heaps, so that the rain may run off more easily without making the heap sodden. The liquid from a manure heap, however, should not be allowed to run waste, as it contains valuable plant foods. If allowed to run into a hollow place at the foot of the heap, the liquid can then be thrown over the manure from time to time, thus preventing it from getting too hot and mouldy.

It sometimes happens, when manure is improperly managed by leaving the rotted and unrotted portions mixed up together without being turned and watered, that a heap catches fire—much in the same way that haystacks do in summer and autumn, owing to the enormous heat generated by decomposition in the interior. Accidents of this kind are very costly, and the only way to prevent a manure heap being totally consumed is to give it a thorough drenching with water.

MAKING THE HOT-BEDS

From October till the end of March hot-beds are in constant use for the production of early crops. As some of these require more heat than others it is necessary to regulate the thickness and heat of the beds according to the season and the crop grown. If the temperature is too high there is great danger of the plants becoming too tender and "sappy" in growth ; they are, therefore, likely to suffer considerably when exposed during the cold winter months. On the other hand, just the right temperature must be maintained to secure the maximum amount of growth in the shortest time, coupled with careful ventilation on all favourable occasions.

French growers usually make three different kinds of beds according to season and crop—namely, (1) raised hot-beds ; (2) sunken beds in trenches for melons ; and (3) in April beds made from spent manure or the dark mould that has already played its part in the production of previous crops.

Having marked out by means of pegs and lines where the beds and frames and cloches are to be placed—bearing in mind that they are to be inclined towards the south, south-east, or south-west—the manure is wheeled on to the ground or carried on the back in the peculiar wicker baskets called " hottes " (see figs. 13, 14, p. 44).

It is the custom to make the beds deeper on a wet, heavy soil than on a warm, light, sandy one, and also to make narrow beds deeper than wide ones. Beds made during the winter months are also thicker in proportion than those made in autumn or spring, as greater heat is required to resist the atmospheric cold.

The most reliable manure for maintaining a good and steady heat is undoubtedly stable manure well moistened with urine. In a fresh state it is rarely used, as the heat generated is much too great, being often as much as 140° to 160° Fahr. Fresh manure is brought into proper condition by turning it over two or three times with a fork. It is then ready for use either by itself when great heat is needed, or mixed with older and less active manure when a lower temperature is required.

French gardeners make their hot-beds about 5 ft. 5 in. in width. This allows 4 ft. 5 in. for the frames, or three rows of cloches on top when arranged as shown in fig. 2. A pathway about 1 ft. wide is thus left between each bed, but it is really only about 9 or 10 in., as the manure must project a little beyond the frames. The length of the beds is regulated by the number of frames used ; but five frames (carrying fifteen lights) are generally placed one after the other before an intersecting pathway is made.

When actually making up the hot-beds the well-mixed manure should be placed in layers over the required space, taking care to keep the edges vertical. When sufficient manure has been placed in position, it should be trodden down well with the feet, and beaten with the fork to secure a level surface and equal density throughout. Any hollow places must be filled up with more manure, until the proper level has been reached. When complete, the whole bed should be watered all over if inclined to be dry, so that it is made moist enough to generate a steady heat.

When making beds in October for the cultivation of Lettuces, they need not be more than 8 in. in depth. A fair quantity of short litter should be mixed with the hot and fresh manure, because at this period the plants do not require heat so much as being kept rather dry and sufficiently warm. Beds made in November should be somewhat deeper, and made with equal parts of old and fresh manure. From the commencement of December the beds should be from 12 to 14 in. thick, and made of fresher manure.

FIG. 2.—SHOWING HOW THREE ROWS OF CLOCHES ARE ARRANGED ON BEDS.

This is necessary, as a greater and more steady heat is then required for such crops as Lettuces, early Carrots, and Turnips.

If the beds are to be covered with cloches, the surface should have a layer of old mould spread over it evenly. After this three rows of cloches are placed upon each bed, alternating as shown in fig. 2.

When the beds are intended to carry frames, these may be placed upon them as soon as made, and when properly arranged in straight rows, the surface of the beds may be covered with mould, or even with finely sifted gritty soil in the springtime. When the frames are in position, the "lights" are placed upon them, and these are covered with mats for a few days to hasten the more rapid heating of the manure in the dark.

In preparing the ground to be occupied by a rang· of beds the work is carried out as follows : The soil is taken out about 3 ft. 3 in. wide at the base and thrown into a raised heap or ridge the length of the range, so as not to hold the water, or to drain itself if already too wet. When the ground for the first row of frames has been treated in this way, the soil from the second row is used for placing on the hot-bed in the first row, the soil from the third is placed in the second, and so on to the last row.

The narrow pathway which has been left between each row of frames at first remains empty if the weather is not too severe. According, however, as the hot-beds begin to lose some of their heat, the pathways between the frames are filled up, or " lined," with short or strawy litter, not short, hot manure. This is moistened by the dripping rain from the lights, and with the heat from the beds, the manure in the pathways gradually generates heat and serves to rekindle or conserve the heat in the beds themselves for a longer period. The ends of the frames are banked up with manure about a foot deep, as are also the sides of the first and last row of the entire range, so that eventually all the frames look as if they were embedded up to the lights in a sea of manure. In this way the frames at the ends of the rows are kept as warm as those in the centre. This is an important consideration, especially for growers who wish to gather an entire crop at once. It is from the wet manure in these narrow pathways that the beds in the frames obtain the necessary moisture during the winter months, by capillary attraction.

When these hot-beds are freshly made and very warm, care should be taken not to sow or plant until the first fierce heat from the manure has somewhat abated. If this precaution is neglected and a very high temperature develops, it may be necessary to take away the outside banks of manure from the frames so as to cool the beds. If this does not suffice, plenty of water must be thrown round the beds and in the pathways until the temperature sinks to the required degree.

COST AND MAINTENANCE OF A FRENCH GARDEN

As much has recently been heard as to the great profits obtainable from an acre or two of ground cultivated on the French system, it may be of interest to consider the approximate cost of establishing a garden, the annual expenditure on the same, and the returns that are likely to be secured from markets in a fairly normal state of trade.

Taking an ordinary French garden devoted mainly to producing early crops, one rarely finds more than 300 frames, or 900 lights, or more than 3,000 cloches. As the frames and lights are moved off one crop on to another, it is advisable to have extra land available so that the changes and rotations necessary may be carried out without difficulty.

Generally speaking, it is more economical in proportion to cultivate two acres than one, as the initial outlay is almost the same in both cases for establishment expenses.

Taking the various items separately for establishment we arrive at the following figures :

TABLE I.—ESTIMATED CAPITAL EXPENDITURE ON TWO ACRES

	£	s.	d.
Water-tank, tower, pumping-engine, stand-pipes, fences, etc., say..	*200	0	0
3,000 Cloches @ £5 per 100	150	0	0
900 Lights, painted and glazed, @ 6/6 each	292	10	0
300 Frames for same @ 8/– each	120	0	0
700 Rye-straw mats @ £5 per 100 ..	35	0	0
Horse, Cart and Harness, say	†60	0	0
6 zinc French waterpots @ 15/– each ..	4	10	0
3 Spades @ 4/6	0	13	6
2 Forks @ 3/6	0	7	0
2 American Rakes, 14 teeth, @ 3/– each..	0	6	0
1 Manure Basket with straps	0	17	6
1 Manure Stand, iron	1	0	0
1 Wheelbarrow	1	0	0
3 Hose pipes, say	6	0	0
Dibbers, lines, tilts, handbarrow, etc., say	1	16	0
Packing Shed, say	20	0	0
Miscellaneous, say	30	0	0
Total	£924	0	0

* If water can be obtained easily and at a specially cheap rate from a water company, there would be no need to go to the expense of sinking a well, erecting a water-tower and tank, or for having a pumping-engine. This sum might, therefore, be reduced by say £150, making the total outlay £774 instead of £924.

† This expense need not be incurred the first year, perhaps, unless it can be well afforded.

TABLE II.—ESTIMATED ANNUAL EXPENSE ON TWO ACRES

	£	s.	d.
Manure, 1,000 tons @ 5/– per ton ..	250	0	0
Labour	260	0	0
Maintenance of Horse (*see* note, p. 25) ..	30	0	0
Rent, Rates, Taxes, Insurance	50	0	0
Miscellaneous Expenses, including cost of Seeds, say	40	0	0
Total	£630	0	0

TABLE III.—ESTIMATED ANNUAL RECEIPTS FROM TWO ACRES

	£	s.	d.
Lettuces, say	250	0	0
Cauliflowers, say	80	0	0
Melons, say	150	0	0
Carrots, say	125	0	0
Radishes, say	125	0	0
Endives, say	25	0	0
Corn Salad, say	10	0	0
Spinach, say..	10	0	0
Cabbages, say	10	0	0
Celery, say	10	0	0
Turnips, say	15	0	0
Asparagus, Dwarf Beans, Cucumbers, Strawberries, Tomatoes, etc., say ..	50	0	0
Total	£860	0	0

BALANCE SHEET

Dr. RECEIPTS.				EXPENSES		*Cr.*	
	£	s.	d.		£	s.	d.
As per Table III.	860	o	o	As per Table II.	630	o	o
				Profit	230	o	o
	£860	o	o		£860	o	o

From the figures given above it will be seen that the expenditure of a French• garden is very great for the first year—£924 sunk in capital, and £630 in expenses, making £1,554 altogether. Out of this sum, however, under proper management and with normal markets, it is estimated that £860 of the outlay would be returned. This represents a profit for the year of £230, or nearly 25 per cent. on the capital. It may therefore be assumed that at the end of four years not only would the capital be paid back, but all expenses would be paid into the bargain. Under exceptionally favourable circumstances, this desirable result may possibly be attained at the end of three years ; but it is difficult to see how it could be accomplished much sooner. On the other hand, if the freehold of the garden is purchased, and a good house be erected on the land, it may possibly take six or eight years to wipe out the capital and expenses, before one can really look upon the results of his work as being pure profit.

It will be understood, of course, that the figures given are only approximate, although the prices of cloches, frames, mats, and tools may be regarded as fairly accurate. Much more money may be spent on these articles, but an ingenious man will find he can economise in many ways. For example, it is possible to make his own frames, to paint and glaze his own lights, to make his own tilts, manure stands, etc. He may also be able to dispense with a horse and cart, although he would probably find this difficult in an out-of-the-way place.

So far as the figures for the produce are concerned, the estimates have been based on rather low average prices in the markets. It has been computed that the produce from each light realises 20s., and from each cloche 2s. On this basis the nine hundred lights given above would yield £900, and the three thousand cloches £300—making £1,200 per annum from these two sources alone. I am inclined to think these figures, however, are too high.

Besides the crops mentioned, there are others that might be looked upon as a source of revenue even in a garden of two acres, such for instance as Strawberries, Tomatoes, Early Potatoes, and some others referred to at pp. 62, 63. It would be safer, however, for the beginner to confine his attention strictly to those crops that can be grown economically in bulk and fetch the best prices. Afterwards, when he feels more sure of his ground, other crops might be grown if considered desirable and sufficiently remunerative.

MARKETING

Perhaps one of the most difficult problems connected with commercial gardening is the disposal of the produce at such a price as to yield reasonable profits. In this connection much depends not only upon the way the " stuff " is grown, but also upon the way it is prepared for sale. It is well known that the very finest produce in the world stands a very poor chance of selling at all, unless it is packed in a neat, cleanly, and attractive way. The almighty greengrocer is often the most important factor to be considered, and his judgment is generally final. Caterers for large establishments also have keen eyes for the way produce is exposed for sale ; and the grower or his agent must not be surprised at any uncomplimentary references to his vegetables and salads if they are not packed in such a way as to command approval or to attract ready and favourable attention. It is therefore of the utmost importance that Lettuces, Carrots, Radishes, Cauliflowers, Turnips, etc., should be prepared for sale and as carefully packed as possible. There are now many kinds of crates, boxes, and baskets in use—some made of willow, others of thin strips of wood, all combining lightness with cheapness and neatness. All root crops like Turnips, Radishes, and Carrots are of course nicely washed and cleaned before or after bunching ; while crops like Cauliflowers, Cabbages, Lettuces, etc., have the roots, stems, and all unnecessary or useless leaves taken away. Each crop indeed is prepared and packed in accordance with what practice has found out to be the best ; but that does not preclude any one from improving upon the present methods, if he sees a reasonable chance of doing so. Originality, combined with neatness and good produce, very often means remarkably quick sales.

If a grower does not go to market himself, or sell direct to his own customers, he must of necessity send his produce to a commission salesman in one

or other of the great markets : and herein lies one
of the great dangers of the business. There are
undoubtedly salesmen of repute in all the best markets
who do their best for their clients in selling at the
highest prices ; and they return these prices to the
grower, less the legitimate commission to which
they are entitled. Notwithstanding this fact, however, it is unfortunately too true that letters appear
frequently in the trade papers from growers who
relate that not only do they receive but little, or
even *nothing*, for the goods sent to the salesman,
but in some cases the latter individual actually sends
in a charge for expenses incurred in disposing of the
produce ! This, coupled with the high railway rates—
which are in themselves equivalent to a protective
tariff—often drives the grower of good produce to
despair. It is rare, however, that one hears of a
commission agent entering the bankruptcy court.

A WORD TO AMATEUR GARDENERS

The figures given in the preceding pages refer to
the establishment and maintenance of a " French
Garden " on strictly commercial and professional
lines, and they may well cause the amateur to pause
before embarking on such a system of cultivation.
Where, however, one has a small piece of ground at
his disposal—say only 10 or 20 poles—there is no
reason why he should not practise the art on a small
scale, and at comparatively little expense. It must
be borne in mind, however, that as the cloches and
lights frequently require attention in regard to closing
and opening (*i.e.* putting on air and taking it off), as
well as shading, the amateur must either be at hand

to attend to these operations himself, or must delegate the duties to some intelligent member of his house-hold. Otherwise his crops are sure to suffer.

In large private establishments (as distinguished from purely commercial ones) the proprietors fre-quently employ gardeners skilled in the production of fruits, flowers, and vegetables. Where these are grown early in hothouses perhaps the system of cloches, hot-beds, and lights will not appeal very strongly. In cases, however, where there is but little or no glass, one might do worse than invest in two or three hundred cloches and a few frames and lights—bearing in mind that there ought to be a good supply of water always available.

It is impossible to estimate exactly the probable outlay and annual expenses that would be incurred by any particular amateur, but as may be seen from the figures below, a good deal could be done by the outlay of £20, and more of course in proportion to what is spent. For a small garden the following estimate may serve as an example :

	£	s.	d.
100 Cloches	6	0	0
6 Frames @ 10/– each	3	0	0
18 Lights @ 7/6 each	6	15	0
18 Mats @ 1/6 each	1	7	0
Tools and Sundry Expenses, say ..	3	0	0
Total Cost of Establishment ..	£20	2	0

The prices quoted are higher than those given on p. 25, as small purchasers usually have to pay more for material than large ones.

The annual expenses incurred in such a garden might be given thus :

	£	s.	d.
Manure, 10 tons @ 6/– per ton	3	0	0
Labour	5	0	0
Sundries	2	0	0
	£10	0	0

These figures are given on the assumption that the amateur attends to the business himself, and employs only occasional labour to help with making the beds, etc.

The produce from the lights and cloches ought to be worth the same price at least to the amateur as it fetches in market. The annual value therefore would be as follows :

	£	s.	d.
Produce of 18 Lights @ 15/– each ..	13	10	0
,, ,, 100 Cloches @ 1/6 each ..	7	10	0
Total	£21	0	0

So that at the end of the first year, having spent £30 altogether, the return would be only £9 short of the total expense. On the same basis, there should be a clear profit of £11 the second and succeeding years, equivalent to 55 per cent. on the capital outlay.

IMPLEMENTS AND ACCESSORIES

For intensive cultivation special appliances are necessary to enable the gardener to secure the best results. The most important will now be considered.

FRAMES.—These are made of deal planks about an inch or more in thickness. Those used at the back are generally 9 in. wide, those in front being an inch or two narrower. Each frame is 13 ft. long and 4 ft. 5 in. wide and is built to take three lights; so that two men can easily move a frame from one place to another. The ends of the frames are often made of oak, and the four planks are nailed together, having a stout oak post at each corner. The back posts are 13 or 14 in.• long, those in front being

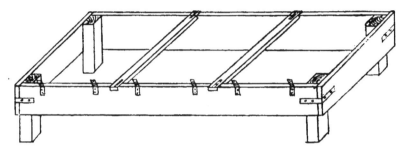

FIG. 3.—A 3-LIGHT FRAME AS USED IN FRENCH GARDENS.

10 or 11 in., the tops in both cases being flush with the upper edge of the boards. This gives a slope to the frames and not only throws off the rain into the pathways, but also catches the rays of the sun better. Movable bars connect back and front planks for supporting the lights in the usual way. With fair wear and tear the frames last about fifteen years. Fig. 3 shows a frame for three lights, the " rests " on the front plank being to prevent the lights slipping off .when lifted up for watering.

LIGHTS.—The size favoured by French growers is 4 ft. 5 in. by 4 ft. 3 in. Where durability and economy are taken into account the frames of the lights are generally made of oak. The bottom rail, however,

is often made of iron, as it is more liable to rot
the water.   In the latest make the sash bars—of
there are three—are also made of iron, and a
narrow as possible, consistent with firmness, so
the maximum amount of light is given to the
when necessary.

The lights are painted and glazed in the
way, except that top-putty is used on iron sash
and the smallest pane of glass is kept at the bo
because it runs greater risk of being broken tha
others ; consequently it is not so difficult or cos
replace.

It may be mentioned that the frames and
in French gardens are narrow for scientific as
as useful reasons.   In winter, when it would be da
ous to water the early crops with cold water
necessary moisture is obtained from the wet m
in the narrow pathways by capillarity.   If the f
were too wide, water would not be attracted s
as the centre of the bed, hence the plants there
suffer from drought.

CLOCHES.—This name for " bell glasses " ha
come almost an English word now, so it ma
retained without inconvenience in this work.   Cl
have been in constant use in French gardens
about the year 1623—nearly three hundred ye
although originally they are said to have come
Italy.   They have naturally undergone conside
modification in that time.   The best cloches are
in Lorraine, and measure about 17 in. in diai
across the mouth, and about 15 in. in l
(see fig. 4).   Each one weighs about $5\frac{1}{2}$ lb.,
will hold about 6 gallons of water.   The cloche

made of clear glass with a slightly bluish tint as a protection against strong sunshine.   Formerly cloches had a knob on top, but as this acted like a lens and burned the plants beneath, those without knobs are now preferred, and generally used.   It has been computed that something like five or six millions are in use in French gardens.   It is con-sidered more economical to order 200 or 300 at one time, as small packages are more liable to be broken in

FIG. 4.—CLOCHE COVERING CABBAGE LETTUCES.

passing from hand to hand.   English glass makers, I believe, are waking up to the fact that there is likely to be a trade in bell-glasses for intensive gardening purposes, so that growers will have an opportunity of encouraging home industries, if the prices are reasonable.

Cloches, being obviously fragile, a good deal of care is necessary in handling them.   They are generally placed in stacks of three, and by means of a specially

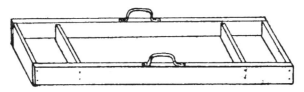

FIG. 5.—CLOCHE CARRIER.

constructed frame one man can carry as many as twelve—weighing about 66 lb.—at one time.   He carries two stacks of three, back to back, in front of him, and two similar stacks behind him on the frame. So that the cloches shall not roll off, the cross-pieces next the man are slightly lower than those at the ends (see fig. 5).

The cloche carrier is only used for long distances. For a short distance a man can easily carry three cloches in each hand by inserting a finger between them.

When the cloches are not in use they are stacked away carefully in piles of any number up to ten. Five, however, is a safer number, as shown in fig. 6. Formerly wisps of straw, hay, or litter were placed between them to prevent breakages. It was found, however, that if the straw became wet the cloches were liable to crack. Now they are placed on firm ground on which some straw or litter has been spread. A small square piece of wood or block, as shown in the figure, is put on the top of the first cloche before the second is placed on it. This prevents one cloche touching the other, and if the work is done properly the upper cloche will turn round easily on the lower. It is hardly necessary to say that the cloches are placed in positions sheltered from strong winds, otherwise an unexpected hurricane might do considerable damage. The stacks of cloches are placed in rows alternating with each other, and as a protection against sudden hailstorms in summer they are covered with straw or old mats. During the winter months it is never wise to place the cloches on their side when not in use, as the side touching the ground is likely to drop out if surprised by a hard frost, and especially if there is any water inside.

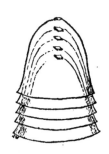

FIG. 6.—CLOCHES STACKED UP WHEN NOT IN USE.

The interior of the cloches is kept clean by washing every year about November, when there is little danger of the sun causing the young plants beneath to flag or " wilt." A wisp of hay, or old rye mat tied in the middle, makes a rough brush for the purpose. The cloche is plunged into a tub of water, and as it is twirled round with one hand the interior is brushed with the other. The glass is then well rinsed and comes out perfectly clean and as good as new. There is no need to wash the •outer surface, as this is kept sufficiently clean by the rain. During the summer months, however, some of the cloches are covered with whiting for shading purposes, but this is easily removed by the hand when washing the glasses.

Occasionally a cloche gets broken, and old French gardeners became experts at putting the pieces together when prices ruled high. Those I have seen in gardens near Paris were mended with strips of linen or pieces of glass and white lead placed over the cracks. Curiously enough a once-broken glass generally has a long life after being mended, as it is handled with more than usual care. Now, however, it is scarcely worth while mending· badly broken cloches, as they are so moderate in price—about £5 to £6 per 100. Some of the special sticking glues like Seccotine would probably be a great improvement on the white lead and linen method.

By the use of cloches the gardener is enabled not only to protect tender plants from the cold and wet during the worst period of the year, but owing to the genial temperature beneath them, he can also raise his plants more quickly than in the open air in the ordinary way. By constant use over the plants,

3 *

having due regard to ventilation and shading, each cloche serves all the purposes of a miniature forcing house.

MATS.—As one might expect, coverings of mats or sacks were in use to protect plants long before even cloches or frames were thought of. In these days the mats mostly in use are made of rye straw. Each

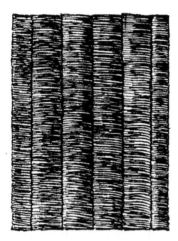 mat is about 5 ft. to 6 ft. 6 in. long, and 4 ft. 6 in. wide, weighs about 11 or 12 lb., and is kept together by means of five strings running across the straw stems (see fig. 7). Before use the mats are steeped in a solution of copper sulphate not only to preserve them, but also to prevent rats and mice from gnawing them, and to keep off fungoid diseases. Each mat costs about 1s. 2d.

FIG. 7.—RYE-STRAW MAT.

to 1s. 6d., and with fair wear and tear ought to last three or four seasons.

The mats are useful not only for protecting the plants in the frames or under the cloches from severe frosts in winter, but in summer time they are almost as much in evidence for shading the lights and cloches from the scorching rays of the sun. Old mats are useful for covering the cloches that are stacked up in summer; to protect them against the sudden hailstorms that often do much damage. Although the rye-straw mats are reasonably cheap, it may be worth while to make them in gardens when bad weather prevents the employees from doing other work.

Boys, girls, or women would probably become more expert at mat-making in a much shorter time than men. A smart willing lad should earn from 30 to 50 per cent. more per day than a man at making mats. A special frame is used for the purpose, but I have seen mats made on the wooden floor of a barn equally well. The frame consists of two pieces of wooden batten 3 or 4 in. wide, and 6 ft. or more in length, as desired. These battens form the side pieces, and are kept the required distance apart by the insertion of two cross battens about 5 ft. long—one at the end, and the other at any desired distance from it, according to the length of the mat. Four or five nails or pegs are stuck into the cross pieces, at equal distances apart, cord or tarred twine is then tightly stretched from one nail to

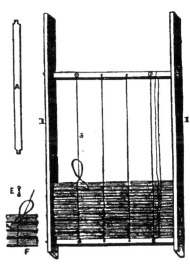

FIG. 8.—FRAME FOR MAKING MATS.

(1) Side boards ; (A) Cross-bar to keep sides equidistant. (5) Strings strained tightly from nails at each end. (E) Reel or bobbin for twine. (F) showing loop made when sewing.

another. The straw is now taken in handfuls and spread evenly across the strings on the frame—the cut ends being pushed against the side battens. Sewing now takes place. A quantity of string or twine is wound on a bobbin or reel about 6 in. long. The string is passed over the straw, under the bottom string, made into a loop knot, and pulled tight, so that each layer of straw is pressed close up and does not exceed three-quarters of an inch in thickness. A similar tie is made at each string, passing always from the centre to one side or the other. Handful after handful of straw is added and sewn in the way described, until a mat of the required length has been made. The mat is then detached, and the strings at each end are knotted up tightly to prevent un-ravelling. Any ragged edges may be cut with shears or scissors.

Where an abundance of straw from rye or wheat is obtainable cheaply, it might well be utilised for making mats. The chief points to bear in mind are to add the same quantity of straw each time and keep it even and regular.

To preserve the mats, they are immersed in a large wooden bath or cement tank, in which a copper sulphate solution has been prepared. This solution is made by dissolving from 6 to 8 lb. of sulphate of copper in 22 gallons of water. When well saturated with the solution, the mats may be taken out and hung up to dry.

FRAME " TILTS."—This is the technical name given to small blocks of wood, or sometimes brickbats or

FIG. 9.—
FRAME TILT.

flower-pots, used for propping up the lights of the frames either at the top or bottom, or on one side or the other. As more air is given at one time than another according to the season, the temperature, and the force of the wind, the tilts, as used in frames, are usually made with two or three notches—so that much or little air can be given at will as shown in fig. 9. The tilt may be used in four different ways: (1) flat on the side,

(2) on the first notch, (3) on the second notch, and (4) on the top notch. When the plants are young and tender the tilt is usually placed on its side. As the plants increase in size and sturdiness, however, a little more air may be given, and notches 1, 2, and 3 are utilised in turn.

To avoid straining the framework of the lights when giving air, the tilt should be placed near the middle of the rail at the side, or at the top or bottom, instead of being nearer to one end or to one side than to the other.

Another important point to remember is, not to tilt the lights on the side facing towards the wind, but on the side away from it. The wind thus passes over the frames without causing a cold draught. Should the lights be raised on the wrong side, the wind enters freely and causes the leaves to " flag " or wilt, and they may perhaps receive a check from which they never recover. Besides, there is another danger from raising the lights on the wrong side, viz. that a strong breeze may easily lift the lights from their position, and break a considerable amount of glass.

It may be as well to mention—although it is well known to practical men—that when plants have been exposed for a week or ten days to the greatest possible amount of air that can be given by the tilt standing upright, they will have become so hardened off that the lights themselves may be taken off altogether on bright genial days. In addition to experience, the state of the weather and the season will, however, guide one as to whether it is safe to leave the lights off during the night time or not.

CLOCHE TILTS.—It is quite as necessary at times

to give air to the plants beneath cloches as it is to those in frames or greenhouses.   Special tilts (called " fourchettes " by the French gardeners) are made

for this.   They consist of a narrow, triangular piece of wood, about 10 or 12 in. long, made out of slating battens or staves, and with a couple of notches taken out at right angles on the longer side, or hypoteneuse, some-what as shown in fig. 10. The pointed end is stuck

FIG. 10.—TILT SHOWING NOTCHES PROPERLY MADE.

FIG. 11.—TILT BADLY MADE.

into the ground and the cloche is lifted so that the rim may rest on either the first or second notch, as shown in fig. 12.

Very often before the cloche is lifted on to the first notch, when the plants are still very young and

FIG. 12.—SHOWING CLOCHE OVER SEEDLINGS, TILTED UP ON ONE SIDE FOR AIR. CLOCHE TILT SHOWN ON RIGHT.

tender, a depression is made close to the rim, by pressing the closed fist into the spongy surface of the bed.

When " air is taken off," that is, when the cloches are let down flat on the bed again, it is done by placing the index finger on top of the tilt and pressing it backwards.   The cloche then drops to the sur-face by its own weight.   In this way it does not occupy much time to " take the air off " a few hundred cloches.

If, however, the cloche tilt is badly made, and has

the notches at any angle *le*ss than a right angle, it will be impossible to take off the air with the finger only, in the way described. Both hands will have to be used, and this means considerable waste of time. A badly-made cloche tilt is shown at fig. 11.

The cloches are, naturally, tilted up on the side away from the wind, and if the tilt is firmly fixed in the soil, there is little danger of the glasses being blown about by ordinary breezes. Sometimes, however, a storm springs up suddenly, and then the damage to the cloches is likely to be great.

HAND-BARROWS.—These are similar to those in use in English nurseries, but have no legs. They are useful for carrying lights, etc., in the narrow alleys between the frames.

MANURE BASKET.—Owing to the fact that the ranges of frames have pathways of a foot or less between them, it is obvious that a man could not use an ordinary wheelbarrow between them for carrying manure or soil. The pathways are narrow chiefly to economise space (owing to the high rents in Paris and the cost of manure), and even the handles of the lights are on top of the rails instead of the ends, so that another inch or two of valuable space may be secured. To enable the gardeners, therefore, to get between the beds and frames, a peculiar shaped wicker basket called a " hotte " is used for carrying manure, etc. This " hotte " (see fig. 13) has almost a straight back, in front of which are two straps which fit over a man's shoulders, so that it is carried much in the same way as a glazier carries his frame and glass, as shown in fig. 14. These baskets hold quite a large quantity of manure—more than a wheelbarrow. While it is being filled, it is placed on a stand called a " chargeoir " (see fig. 14). This is a tripod, made of wood or iron, having two upright posts or horns, one at each end of the platform. This is at a convenient height from the ground, so that there is no

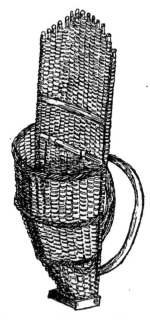

FIG. 13.—WICKER MANURE BASKET WITH STRAPS.

FIG. 14.—SHOWING MAN ABOUT TO CARRY A BASKET CHARGED WITH MANURE FROM STAND.

necessity for a man to stoop or rise when he wishes to take the laden basket on his shoulders. He simply places his back to the basket, arranges the straps over his shoulders, and marches off to the spot where the manure is wanted. To march steadily and quickly in an alley, about a foot wide, between rows of frames, with a couple of hundredweights of manure on the back, necessitates a good deal of skill which can only be acquired by practice. Having reached his destination, the workman tilts his basket to the right or left, and shoots the manure from it almost exactly in the same way as a coalheaver gets rid of his sack of coals.

MISCELLANEOUS IMPLEMENTS.—In addition to the above, other tools will be required. Amongst those most generally useful will be found steel spades, shovels, dung forks and digging forks, iron rakes (of which the American pattern is best), dibbers and trowels for transplanting, line and reel, and other odds and ends that will suggest themselves from time to time.

THERMOMETERS are almost indispensable in a " French " garden so that one may see at a glance whether the temperature is too high or too low for a specific purpose. Hot-bed or plunge thermometers are particularly useful, as it is easy, especially for beginners, to misjudge the heat of a bed—and mis-judgment may mean a serious loss at times.

As all gardeners must constantly keep an eye upon " the weather, and the setting of the winds," a good barometer in the house will always be found of the greatest use, in addition to the thermometers.

WATER-POTS.—These indispensable adjuncts to a garden vary much in shape and size, and those used in France are built on somewhat different lines from those used in this country. The French gardeners prefer water-pots as shown in fig. 15, from which it will be seen that the strong, curved handle runs from near the base of the can on one side to the ex-treme margin on the other. This style of handle enables the gardener to use two water-pots—one in each hand—without having to put them down for refilling. When carrying water the handle is held

on top right over the body of the can. When, however, water is being poured from the spout, the gardener,
with an expert jerk, brings his hands farther back
along the handle. This naturally sends the water
out of the spout with force, and thus the water-pot
in each hand can be emptied without placing it on
the ground. When empty, the cans are slid or jerked
back into a vertical position, and filled and emptied
again in the same way as often as necessary.

FIG. 15.—FRENCH WATER-POT WITH SEMI-CIRCULAR HANDLE AND LARGE
" ROSE " TO SPOUT.

The best water-pots are made in copper, and last
a life-time—indeed, they almost become heir-looms.
They cost from 25s. to 30s. a pair, each one holding
about 2½ to 3 gallons of water. English growers will
probably prefer their own water-pots, which they
can handle just as dexterously as the Frenchman
handles his.

The long-handled spades, or shovels, and forks are
not likely to commend themselves to English gardeners
who have been so long accustomed to the loop-handled
tools. They are, however, specially suitable **for**

French gardening. It certainly appears much easier to fill a manure-basket with a long-handled fork than with a short one, and the long-handled spade or shovel is a convenience when filling the frames with soil.

WATERING

Under ordinary conditions the proper application of water to the roots of plants requires a good deal of care and judgment, as every professional gardener knows. When, however, plants are grown under forced conditions under cloches and lights on hot-beds, it is more than ever essential that watering should be done carefully and judiciously. All plants do not absorb water from the soil at the same rate. The roots of some kinds are much more active than those of others ; consequently, the gardener must have this knowledge " at the back of his head " whenever he waters his crops. The temperature, both outside and inside the frames and cloches, must be taken into account, also the particular period of the year, and the weather actually prevailing at the time. Sometimes an abundance of water will be given, but on other occasions perhaps a mere sprinkling overhead will suffice for the same crops. Over-watering—*i.e.* giving too much—must be just as carefully avoided as under-watering, or not giving sufficient when the plants need it. In the case of over-watering the soil or mould is apt to become sour and sodden, fresh air is excluded, the tender roots perish through suffocation or absence of oxygen, or the lower leaves are attacked with some fungoid disease which sets up rapid discoloration and decay throughout the entire plant. On the other hand, a lack of water at the roots causes the leaves to droop or " flag," in which condition they are unable to assimilate even the small amount of carbonic acid gas floating in the atmosphere, or to perform their other functions properly.   The result may be to induce the plants to " bolt " into flower prematurely.   To strike the happy medium, therefore, is the constant aim of the cultivator, and this can only be done by exercising his intellectual faculties and making use of the knowledge he has already acquired.

WATERING IN WINTER.—So far as early crops or " primeurs " of Carrots, Radishes, Lettuces, Cauli-flowers, etc., are concerned, no water, as water, is actually applied to the hot-beds on which they are raised or growing from January to March.   These early crops secure sufficient moisture from the damp, hot manure beneath them, and this obtains its supplies by capillary attraction from the rains that run into the narrow pathways from the lights.   It thus becomes necessary to open the lights only when absolutely needful, and the danger of chilling the plants by cold water is thus avoided during the coldest period of the year.

In the spring and early summer, and then onwards during the growing season, the application of water becomes an important feature in the day's work. Generally speaking, it is best to give water either in the mornings before ten o'clock, or in the afternoon after three, four, or five o'clock, according to circumstances and convenience.   Watering should always be avoided during the middle of the day when the sun is very hot.   Tender-leaved plants especially are liable to be severely scorched and spoiled by having water upon them at this time, especially if any happen to be under a cloche or light, as the glass in either case acts as a lens, and concentrates the rays of the sun upon certain portions of the leaf surface.

When crops are well established and in full growth during the summer months, water is applied freely by means of a hose attached to the nozzle of a stand-pipe. Standpipes should be fixed about every 20 or 30 ft. to the 2 in. or 3 in. water-pipes running underground along the main pathways. This enables one to attach the hose to the nozzle of the most convenient standpipe, and if the latter is provided with a good screw-valve, the flow and force of water can be easily regulated.

In French market-gardens an ingenious contrivance is used to prevent long lengths of hose from trailing over the plants in the beds or frames. An iron stand, something like the capital letter H in shape, is pressed into the soil at the corner of a bed or row of frames. On the two upper arms, and on the cross-piece, is a movable metal reel. The hose-pipe rests on the cross-piece, and as it is pulled along, its progress is made easy by the movement of the reels. In this way, no matter how sharp the turn or bend, the hose-pipe does not " kink," and the free flow of water is in no way checked.

SEED-SOWING

Under the headings of the various crops mentioned in this book instructions are given as to sowing the seeds in each instance. It may be well, however, to speak of seed-sowing in general a little more fully here.

4

Seeds vary much in size, shape, and colour, but most of those we are dealing with may be described as " small "—the only large ones of any note being those of the Dwarf or French, and Haricot Beans.

No matter how small a seed may be, it contains all the rudiments of the future plant tightly packed away within its protecting coats. So long as the seed is alive and has been properly ripened, it possesses all the powers of germination or sprouting. It is a matter of common knowledge, however, that certain conditions are essential to induce seeds of any kind to germinate. These are : (1) a certain degree of warmth, according to the natural requirements of the species ; (2) moisture ; and (3) fresh air. When these conditions exist in conjunction with a properly prepared compost, we have everything essential for the good germination of seeds.

Even with these conditions there is a danger that young plants may never appear if the seeds are sown improperly. This danger arises only when the seeds are buried too deeply in the soil. One must, therefore, be careful that the smaller the seeds are the less deeply should they be sown ; in other words, they must not be covered with too much soil. A good general rule amongst gardeners when sowing seeds in warmth is to cover them with a layer of soil equal to twice their own diameter. Some tiny seeds, therefore, are practically not covered at all, as they sink sufficiently deep into the miniature holes in the surface of the prepared compost after a gentle watering has been given. Seeds sown in the open air in early spring, or in autumn, however, may be covered rather more heavily as a protection against cold nights or frosts.

It is obvious that if the seeds are not to be covered with too much soil, the beds upon which they are sown must be carefully prepared, and the particles of soil must be rendered sufficiently fine by passing through a sieve. In addition to this, the seed-bed must be made firm by pressing down with a piece of board, or even by treading down with the feet, afterwards finishing off the surface as level as possible by passing a straight-edged board over it, and even by patting it down gently with the flat side. The seeds are thus prevented from sinking too deeply into the soil, and when they germinate the seed-leaves soon reach the light and air from which they draw their food and energy.

Whether the seeds are to be sown in tiny furrows, called " drills," or scattered more or less evenly over the surface " broadcast," depends upon circumstances. As a rule such root crops as Carrots and Turnips are sown in " drills," while Radishes may be sown in drills, or broadcast, or even in patches between other crops. The different ways in which the various seeds are to be sown are mentioned under each particular crop.

In " intensive " cultivation it is essential to sow seeds evenly and thinly as a rule, to save trouble later on, although it is generally permissible to sow much thicker than in the open ground.

THINNING OUT.—With crops like Carrots, Turnips, and Radishes that are grown for their " roots," it is detrimental to lift the seedlings and transplant them to another place. All the roots would be spoiled by doing so ; they would become " fanged " or " forked," instead of being symmetrically shaped, owing chiefly to the original tap-root being injured by moving, no matter how carefully done.   Such root-crops, therefore, are allowed to mature in the spot where the seeds are sown.   If the young plants, however, are too close together, they suffer sooner or later, owing to lack of air and light.   Hence it becomes necessary to pull out the weakest seedlings, thus allowing more root space and air space for the sturdier plants.   This is called " thinning out."

PRICKING OUT.—Crops that are not grown for their roots, but for their heads, such as Cauliflowers, Lettuces, Cabbages, etc., are generally moved from the bed in which the seeds are sown.   This moving is an advantage, as more root fibres—and consequently more feeding agents—are thus produced, and more nourishment is absorbed in a given time from the soil than would be the case with an unmoved plant.

In   " intensive "   cultivation,   French   market-gardeners do not leave their seedlings so long in the seed-bed as is customary in England.   Soon after the first true leaves appear beyond the seed-leaves, or cotyledons, the baby seedlings are " pricked out " into prepared beds, either in frames or under cloches. They are then gently watered, shaded from strong sunshine for two or three days, during which period also no outer air is admitted.   This method ensures the more rapid establishment of the young plants, which consequently come earlier to a state of maturity.

When French gardeners are pricking out seedlings of Lettuces, Cauliflowers, etc., on the soft beds, they rarely use a dibber or stick.   The index-finger is used instead for making holes in the compost, and it is astonishing how rapidly seedling after seedling is put into its place and made firm with the fingers. The French gardener literally carries a dibber at the tips of his fingers, and he nearly always inserts the plant right up to lower leaves or seed-leaves.

TRANSPLANTING.—Sometimes—as will be noted from time to time in the following pages—seedlings are moved a second time before they are placed in their final positions. In such cases, however, they are considerably larger, and the roots will have branched further into the soil in all directions. Under these conditions, each plant is carefully lifted with a " ball of soil " attached to the roots. It is then placed in position with the aid of a trowel—the lower leaves just on the surface of the ground—and the new soil is pressed firmly round the base of the plant and the roots.

SHADING AND VENTILATION

These two operations almost go hand in hand, and a good deal of common sense is necessary to enable the gardener to know exactly when to do one or the other or both.

As a rule, young seedlings that are just pricked out or transplanted are shaded from strong sunshine by covering the lights or cloches with mats. At this particular period, when the plants have been more or less injured at the roots by lifting, it is advisable to check the evaporation of moisture or vapour from the millions of minute breathing pores on the surfaces of the leaves. As evaporation goes on more rapidly in sunlight and in a dry atmosphere than it does in the shade and in a moist atmosphere, it is obvious

4 *

that the latter conditions are most likely to help plants, as the injured roots for the time being are unable to suck up moisture from the surrounding soil. These injured roots, however, soon heal up under normal conditions, and masses of new fibres develop behind the injured tips of the older roots. In this way, after the temporary check, the plants are really better off than they were before, by having more feeding roots, and the effect is soon apparent by the way the leaves stand up, and by the development of fresh growths. When the gardener sees this he knows the plants have established themselves in their new home. Therefore he removes the shading material, except perhaps when he considers the sun to be still too powerful.

When freshly moved seedlings are shaded from the sun, the frames or cloches also are shut down tightly. In this way the moisture or vapour arising from the soil is prevented from escaping. It is kept in the air immediately round the leaves and stems of the young plants, and thus prevents the sap in the tissues from being given off freely into the atmosphere. When the lights and cloches are kept shut down in the way described, the plants are said to be kept " close "—meaning that the outer air is not allowed to circulate freely about them for a certain time. Once, however, the plants are again in a growing condition, or have " picked up " as gardeners say, it is essential to allow them as much air and light as possible, consistent with the necessary warmth and moisture. Otherwise they would become weak and lanky—" drawn," as the saying is—and the tissues would be so soft, tender, and flabby, that the plants would be quite useless for any purpose—scarcely fit for rabbit food even.

When growing Lettuces, Cauliflowers, Carrots, Radishes and other crops mentioned in the following pages under lights or cloches, the gardener will at once recognise the great importance of giving light and air at exactly the right moments, in accordance with the instructions given ; and in doing so he must always take the state of the weather into account.

By using the tilts (see figs. 9 to 12) for lights and cloches, or even bricks or blocks of wood, as much or as little air may be given as desired. On very cold days, perhaps only a " crack " of air, as gardeners say, is given by placing the tilts on the lowest notch or on the thinnest side ; and even then perhaps no air will be given until near mid-day—just for an hour or so according to climatic conditions. On other occasions, such as a bright balmy morning, air may be given quite early, and perhaps the cloches or lights will be opened to the full extent of the tilts used. This is called " putting on full air."

Whether much or little air is given, it is always advisable, as already stated, to note the direction of the wind. The tilt is then placed on the opposite side of the cloche or light, so that the draught does not blow directly on to the tender heads of the plants, but passes over them without causing a chill, and a possible check to the growth.

COMBINATION AND ROTATION CROPS

One of the most interesting and striking features of intensive cultivation is the way in which the same piece of ground is made to carry several crops in the course of a season. The crops are generally dissimilar in vegetation, and to secure the best results quick-growing plants are grown with those of a slower development. Thus it is usual to sow Early Radishes and Carrots on the same bed, and to plant Lettuces over them. The Radishes germinate quickly and do not interfere with the slower-growing Carrots, as they are taken off before the latter reach any size. The Lettuces on the same bed have grown into saleable produce in the meantime, and when they are gathered, the Carrots then have the soil, air, and light to themselves—but very often the borders of the beds are planted with Cauliflowers, which mature after the Carrots have been pulled.

Even in the open air this system of combination crops is generally practised. I have seen in the neighbourhood of Vitry ground covered with Lettuces and Endives in various stages of growth, and between the rows quick catch-crops like Spinach and Radishes have been sown. Before these attain any great height, the other crops will have been taken off the ground.

In the following pages numerous examples of combination crops, and intercropping, are given, and there can be no doubt that, practised judiciously, the system has much to recommend it. At no season of the year need the ground be without a crop of some kind.

The principle underlying the " rotation of crops " is also carried out regularly in gardens devoted to intensive cultivation. Thus, the ground which this year, perhaps, is carrying crops of Carrots, Cauliflowers, Lettuces, Radishes, Endives, Spinach, etc., etc., will be utilised next year for the production of Melons, and open-air crops generally, and *vice ve*rsa. In this way a certain portion of the garden is always more or less exposed to the weather, and is kept "sweet" and in good condition for other crops, by the fresh air circulating amongst its particulars.

THE VEGETABLE MARKET IN PARIS

In a volume devoted to the French system of gardening, it may not be out of place to refer to the produce that is sent to the markets of the French capital. The differences in taste and custom between the French and English peoples naturally result in totally different kinds of fruits and vegetables being grown for commercial purposes. What the French market-gardener therefore finds to be a remunerative crop in his own market, the English grower would most likely discover to be a drug in Covent Garden, or in any of the large provincial markets in the kingdom. From the following remarks of mine, in the *American Florist*, the reader may readily see how very different the vegetable produce in the Paris market is from that generally sent to Covent Garden :

" Almost in the centre of Paris on the north bank of the Seine, and opposite the famous church of St. Eustache, are to be found the famous markets of Paris known as the Halles Centrales. Meat, fish, poultry, fruits, flowers and vegetables are all to be found beneath the roof of the famous building erected by Baltard in 1874, which embraces altogether an area of about 22 acres. To see the markets at their best, a visit should be paid about five o'clock in the morning. Amongst horticultural produce, the vegetables seem to be of far more importance here than either the fruits or flowers. Most of the business in the vegetable market is done by women, and row after row of stalls are laden with produce sent in from the market-gardens all round the city.

" There is a general similarity between the Halles Centrales and Covent Garden, London, so far as noise, bustle, and activity are concerned, but there is a great difference in the produce displayed for sale. Vegetables that one rarely sees in Covent Garden, such as Aubergines, Butter Beans, Black Radishes, Haricots Verts, Cantaloup Melons, etc., are greatly in evidence in Paris, and it is evident that a flourishing trade is done in produce that would probably fail to find a customer in London. Salads always constitute a large proportion of the vegetable market in Paris, where, of course, the marketing is largely in the hands of the mothers and daughters of the various families who deal direct with the growers.

" At the time of my last visit to the Central Markets I was particularly struck with the large quantities of Globe Artichokes on sale. They were on every stall, and were selling for about 6d. to 1s. a dozen heads. Mushrooms also were in fair abundance and were realising about 8d. to 9d. per pound. A rather long tapering turnip known as ' Croissy ' was in great abundance, and although it has been grown by Parisian market-gardeners for several generations, it is still considered one of the best all-round varieties. Radishes, the small red varieties with white tips, were of course in evidence everywhere, and they looked so nice and fresh and enticing that it is no wonder they sell in enormous quantities. The Melons of the Cantaloup Prescott variety were on almost every stall, but they were cheap in comparison with what they had realised earlier in the season. Indeed, the street hawkers had barrow-loads of these Melons which they sold in portions at the rate of 2d. or 3d. a pound to passers-by during August.

" Carrots, the short' stump-rooted varieties, are always great favourites in Paris, while there was also an abundance of Golden Celery, Cauliflowers, Sorrel, Garlic, Endive, and Lettuces. I was rather struck with the quantity of small green Vegetable Marrows offered for sale. The fruits were not more than 6 or 7 in. long and were obviously as fresh as they could well be. I was informed that they sold remarkably well, as also did the small Prickly Cucumbers known as ' cornichons.' White-fruited Cucumbers were fairly conspicuous, and as they are not extensively grown, they realise fairly good prices. The long green-fruited Cucumbers are, however, the most highly appreciated. The Black Radishes, which look like intermediate carrots or Croissy turnips that have been smothered in soot, cannot fail to attract attention. All over Paris these curious-looking vegetables were to be seen in the greengrocers' shops."

EXTENSION OF THE FRENCH SYSTEM

Although the French system of intensive cultivation is regarded as being confined to the production of vegetables and salads, there is no reason why the cloches and frames in use may not be turned to good account in connection with other crops. From the nature of the implements, it is obvious that short-stemmed or dwarf-growing crops are likely to lend themselves successfully to the treatment, and the following may be regarded chiefly in the light of suggestions.

1. Strawberries.—Amongst important fruits, Strawberries may be looked upon as being particularly suited for growing under lights or cloches to produce early crops. At present these are grown in pots in greenhouses, close to the glass, and require considerable time and attention in regard to watering, syringing, regulation of temperature, and keeping free from mildew. Grown under cloches, or in beds that will accommodate the frames and lights used for salads, it would be possible to secure early crops of Strawberries in spring from young plantations without going to the trouble of lifting the plants and potting them in the autumn. For instance, in the case of beds, it would be possible after placing the frames and lights over the plants, to fill in the pathways with manure from which heat would be generated in the frames in accordance with the requirements of the season. A certain amount of the short, warm manure could also be worked in between the rows of plants without disturbing the roots, and when the fruits were swelling, a layer of clean litter could be added for the sake of cleanliness. In this way the Strawberries would come into bearing more quickly, and watering and ventilation could be attended to without inconvenience. Once the fruits are gathered, the frames and lights, and manure in the pathways, may be used for other pur-

poses. Of course Strawberries grown in pots could also be forced in the frames if necessary.

Cloches would be found useful for placing over the crowns of the Strawberry plants, if these were planted in three angled rows in the same way as Lettuces, as shown in fig. 41. Each plant would have a cloche to itself, and in cold weather warm manure could be packed in between and around the glasses to keep the plants warm. Later on, when the weather became warmer, it might be possible to have a Cos or Cabbage Lettuce planted in the spaces between the cloches ; and these would probably be useful afterwards for placing over the Lettuces, according to the season.

2. **Tomatoes.**—In most parts of the kingdom it is dangerous to place Tomato plants in the open air till the end of May or early in June, owing to the frosts and cold nights. If, however, hot-beds of the regulation width to accommodate three rows of cloches were prepared, and a gentle heat from the manure were secured, it would be quite possible to sow Tomato seeds under a cloche or two as early as January or February, in the gritty mould that would be placed over the manure. The strongest plants would be pricked out in due course, and after becoming established, air would be given more or less freely by tilting the cloches on all favourable occasions. This would keep the young plants sturdy and actively growing at the same time. If by chance they grew too tall for the cloches before it was safe to dispense with the latter (one being placed under each as soon as possible), the glasses could be raised on three tilts, bricks, or blocks of wood, in the way described for Cucumbers at p. 128. When frost is no longer feared, the cloches

may be dispensed with, and the plants will continue to develop and ripen their fruits without having to undergo the usual check to the roots caused by moving. The plants, of course, should be staked, and during the season all the side shoots (" laterals ") from the main stems should be pinched out when they appear. Only four trusses of flowers should be allowed to set their fruits. The tops should be cut off about two leaves beyond the upper truss of flowers. The leaves, however, should *not* be cut off or mutilated in any way, except when they turn yellow at the base . of the plant.

3. **Early Potatoes.**—Where these are valued it ought not to be difficult to secure a good crop early in the year, with the aid of cloches and frames, and warm manure, the operations being much the same as described for Tomatoes—except, of course, that tubers instead of seeds are being dealt with.

4. **Marrows.**—These are an important crop when the fruits can be secured early in the season. The Bush Marrows, as well as the creeping kinds, might be very easily established early in the year in the following way: About February, or early in March, dig out a few spadefuls of soil where each plant is to grow. The hole thus made should be filled with a layer about a foot thick of hot manure, and covered with about 6 in. of nice, rich, gritty mould. When the rank heat, if any, has subsided and the temperature is about 70° to 75° Fahr., two or three Marrow seeds should be sown about 2 in. deep in the centre of each little bed, and after being watered in, should be covered with a cloche. As many little hot-beds as are required can be made in this way, allowing enough

space between each for the development of the plants later on. After germination air is given as freely as possible, considering the weather, and by the middle or end of May, or before that period in many parts, it will be possible to remove the cloches altogether. Attention to copious waterings and pinching the shoots afterwards constitute the chief cultural details to secure an abundance of early Marrows.

5. **Mint.**—This is another useful and highly appreciated crop when it comes in with the early Potatoes and Green Peas. It could be grown quite easily in the hot-beds in the frames, and could be forced into tender growth as early as required by lining the frames with warm manure if necessary.

6. **Rhubarb.**—Where one can draw upon a plantation of Rhubarb, clumps may be lifted for forcing from December till the end of March, as the young and highly coloured leaved-stalks often realise good prices at this period of the year. For lifted clumps the process of forcing is almost precisely the same as described at p. 76 for the production of green Asparagus, the one essential difference being that the Rhubarb should be grown in the dark. Rhubarb may also be forced without lifting, in the same way as described for White Asparagus (see p. 73). The varieties called " Linnæus," " Champagne," and " Myatt's Victoria " are the best for forcing.

7. **Violets.**—Passing to flowers, perhaps the single-flowered and double-flowered varieties of Violets may be regarded as a good commercial crop early in the season, owing to their delicious fragrance. The general custom is to lift the clumps early in autumn and replant in frames of rich soil. This operation might

be carried out in the same way with hot-beds, but later in the year altogether. It would also be possible to have the Violet-beds arranged so that they could be easily covered with frames and lights, or cloches, without the plants being moved at all. Indeed, the treatment described for obtaining early Strawberries (see p. 60) might be carried out with advantage in the cultivation of early Violets; and with good annual mulchings of manure and plenty of water when required the plants would continue to yield large crops of blossoms for years.

8. **Christmas Roses** (*Helleborus niger*).—During December and January large numbers of these pure white blossoms find their way to market and are highly appreciated. To secure these, the clumps have to be lifted and carried into a warm greenhouse to open their blossoms. If, however, the beds on which they are grown were to be only the width of the frames and lights, it would be an easy matter to force them into early blossom by filling up the pathways between the frames with hot manure, in the same way as for Strawberries (p. 60). With cloches, however, it would be possible to cover each crown, and place the manure between. As great heat is not necessary, the Christmas Rose seems to be particularly well suited for this system of cultivation.

9. **Miscellaneous.**—Several other popular plants, such as early Tulips, Lilies of the Valley, Primroses, Polyanthuses, Auriculas, Forget-me-Nots, etc., might be brought earlier into blossom if desired by the judicious use of frames and cloches.

During July and August, when the lights and cloches are usually stacked away in heaps and piles in French gardens, many of them might be utilised for the propagation of Roses and other beautiful, shrubby plants from the half-ripened summer shoots. Indeed, it is possible, with the enormous varieties of plants now in cultivation, that there are many different ways still unthought of, to which the use of the frame and cloche may be extended. It should, however, be borne in mind that excursions into these other branches of gardening would necessitate more land, labour, etc., and the results might not be worth the trouble in all cases.

PART II

SPECIAL CULTURES DESCRIBED IN ALPHABETICAL ORDER

IN this portion of the work the various methods of culture practised in French gardens is detailed. Each crop is dealt with separately, so that its special needs may not be overlooked. While the functions of all green-leaved plants are the same, it is important for the gardener to bear in mind that many modifications of general principles are rendered necessary according to the period of the year at which he desires his crops to mature. Thus, what may be perfectly sound practice in January and December, may be quite erroneous in June and July. The state of the weather and the various seasons must always be taken into account, and conditions have to be modified almost with every rise and fall in the barometer. Rain, snow, hail, frost, sun, and wind—all have important influences on vegetation, and the intelligent cultivator must keep a steady eye on these to see that his special cultures are in no way adversely affected. He must be, in fact, a kind of weather-prophet and be able to gauge climatic changes with a fair amount of accuracy if he is to succeed.

GLOBE ARTICHOKES

There are many varieties of Globe Artichokes (*Cynara Scolymus*), but the Parisian market-gardeners prefer the one called *Gros Vert de Laon*. Another variety, called *Camus de Bretagne,* is grown in Brittany, and is often eaten in an uncooked state. Other kinds are grown in the middle and south of France that would be quite unsuitable for either a Parisian or English climate.

Globe Artichokes may be raised from seeds, but are more generally increased by carefully detaching suckers from the old roots in March or April. The suckers are planted in a warm bed, and if kept watered as required, they soon make nice plants fit for the open air. The soil should be rich, deeply dug, and well manured. During the summer months the plants should be given plenty of water at the roots if particularly fine heads are desired. This, coupled with abundance of manure and the frequent use of the hoe, constitute the chief features of cultural care.

Although not grown in England at present to such an extent as in France, there is no reason why the taste for the floral bracts of the Globe Artichoke should not increase.

When it is desired to force the plants, the operation is performed much in the same way as described for Asparagus (see p. 76). The plants are taken up carefully in November, and placed in a hot-bed, the heat of which is maintained, if necessary, by lining the frames with hot manure.

ASPARAGUS

Although each year Asparagus (*Asparagus officinalis*) is becoming more and more popular in the British Islands, its consumption is chiefly confined to those who are in no danger of receiving an old age pension from the Government. In France it is otherwise. Almost every one, even the cottager, eats Asparagus— and such Asparagus ! thick, succulent, well-flavoured shoots.

That fine Asparagus can be grown in the British Islands there is no doubt whatever. It is not a matter of soil and climate. In either respect we are quite as well off as our French brethren. It is simply a question of careful attention to the minor details of cultivation that enables the French gardener to produce, even on comparatively poor soil, some of the finest Asparagus in the world. There are three methods of growing Asparagus in French gardens, the culture on a large scale of course being carried on quite apart from that of early salads and vegetables. First of all, there is what is known as " white " or " blanched " Asparagus ; then " green " Asparagus ; after which comes the " Argenteuil " Asparagus.

White Asparagus.—*Raising the Plants.*—To secure good Asparagus it is essential in the first place to obtain seeds of a good strain from a reliable source. The roots that produce clean, thick, well-formed shoots, terminating in a good point that colours easily, are those from which seeds should be saved when ripe. The best variety for the purpose is *Early Argenteuil.*

The seeds are sown about the middle of January on a

nicely prepared hot-bed under lights, and sufficiently thick to allow of a second selection being made later on.

When the young plants are a few inches high, the very best are selected and carefully pricked out in another frame 2 or 3 in. apart. This will admit about three or four hundred plants under each light. After a gentle watering, the young plants are kept " close " for a few days, after which a little air may be given on all fine days. As the season advances, more and more air may be given, until at length, say about May, the lights may be taken off altogether when frosts are no longer feared. Previous to this, care must be taken to protect the plants from frost during the night by spreading mats or litter over the lights when necessary.

Planting.—About the middle of July these young plants will be ready for planting in their final quarters. At this period it will be easy to distinguish the finest-looking plants ; and these only should be chosen for the plantation. To secure a sufficient supply, it is necessary to sow larger quantities of seed and to prick out more plants than are actually needed, so that there may be no difficulty in making a good selection the first year.

Experienced growers have remarked that clumps which produce thin shoots at first continue to do so year after year. Such shoots are produced more freely than the larger and more succulent ones, it is true ; but one fat shoot is more highly valued than five thin ones. Besides, there is more sense in growing the best and most saleable shoots, as their cultivation entails no more attention than the poorer kinds.

5 *

The soil in which the Asparagus plants are to be placed should if possible be light, rich, deeply trenched and well manured in advance. It should also slope more or less towards the south so as to receive the full benefit from the sun.

Intercropping.—The ground between the young plants is not left idle. Short Carrots, Lettuces, Spinach, Corn Salad, Radishes, or any other dwarf and quick-growing crop may be grown between the rows without the slightest danger to the Asparagus. Even Cabbages and Cauliflowers may be grown on the edges of each bed, and in the pathways between them —each crop, of course, at its proper season. The necessary hoeings and waterings that must be given these crops, instead of being detrimental to the young Asparagus, are in reality of great benefit, so much so that very often they make as much progress in one season as Asparagus plants grown in the ordinary way in the open air do in two or three seasons.

After the plants have flowered, no seed capsules are allowed to form, as they exhaust a certain amount of reserve material from the tissues. About the end of October or in November the stems are cut down within an inch or two of the soil, the surface of which is hoed or lightly pricked up with the fork. A good layer of fine rich soil is then spread over the bed, and on this again a good layer of manure. Each autumn this work is renewed to give a fresh supply of nourishment to the roots.

As the plants will be ready for forcing at the end of two years' growth, although it is better to wait till the end of the third year, it is advisable to mark out the beds wide enough to accommodate the frames and lights which are to go over them. The length of these beds will, of course, be determined according to the extent of the ground or the requirements of the grower. As a rule the beds are 4 ft. 5 in. in width, as this is the usual size of the frames and lights used. The beds should run lengthways from east to west, so that the lights will slope towards the south ; and it will be found more convenient if each bed does not exceed 100 ft. in length.

Between one Asparagus bed and another a pathway

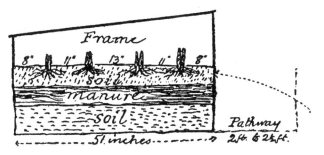

FIG. 16.—FORCING ASPARAGUS IN FRAMES.

about 2 ft. or 2 ft. 6 in. in width should be left (see fig. 16).

Having marked out the Asparagus beds by lines or pegs, about a foot of soil is taken off the surface of the first one, and wheeled to the end of the last bed. The trench thus made is then filled in with a mixture of good horse and cow manure, and, if possible, a little night soil—all of which should have been prepared three or four weeks beforehand, and should be in a half-decomposed and homogeneous condition. In " light " soils the quantity of cow manure may be increased a little, but in " heavy " soils the horse manure should predominate. With this manure many growers mix also old rags, horn-shavings, shoddy, etc.—taking care, however, not to add too much. The manure in the trenches having been trodden down well with the feet, so that it is about a foot thick, about 6 or 8 in. of soil from the adjoining bed is then spread evenly over the surface.

Four rows are marked out in the bed lengthways. The two outer rows are about 8 in. from each margin, the two centre ones being about 13 in. apart. If wider or narrower frames are used the distance between the rows would be regulated accordingly ; but in any case it would be necessary to keep the two outer rows at least 8 or 9 in. away from the edges of the beds.

Transplanting.—Everything being now ready, so far as the beds are concerned, one may proceed to lift the young plants from the bed in which they were pricked out from the seed-bed. It may be advisable, however, to give them a good soaking an hour or two beforehand so that they may be lifted more easily and with some soil still adhering to the roots. Having lifted them carefully with a fork, a selection of the very best plants is again made. From twelve to twenty " crowns " or clumps may be placed in each light—although sixteen is recommended as the best number.

If the frames have not been placed in position before the actual planting, it will be necessary to allow more space between the plants at the end of one frame and the beginning of the next. For this reason it is perhaps advisable to place the frames temporarily in position as soon as the beds have been made. One can then arrange the plants in the rows so that the Asparagus crowns do not come directly under the division or sash bars, but are properly placed beneath the glass itself.

In the spot where each plant is to be placed, a little heap of soil is made with the hands, so as to fill the cavity on the under-side of the crown, and permit the roots being spread out in all directions from the centre. After this, it is only necessary to cover the crowns with fine rich soil to a depth of 3 or 4 in., and then give the whole a good soaking with water.

The young plants soon commence to make new growths, and only require to be kept free from weeds, in addition to which the stems should be tied up to sticks if necessary.

Forcing White Asparagus.—When the young plants have finished their second—or preferably their third—season of growth, they will be sufficiently strong to stand being forced into early growth. This takes place from November to February, although some growers commence as early as the middle of October.

The work is carried out as follows: Having placed the frames on the beds which are to be forced, a layer of fine rich soil and old manure is spread over the plants. The pathways are then dug out to a depth of 12 to 18 in. The soil thus obtained is broken up into a fine condition with the spade or the fork, and is spread evenly over the mould in the frames to a depth of 10 or 12 in. This is done to secure longer and finer stalks later on.

The sunken pathways are now filled up with good fresh manure that has been turned over two or three times in advance. This manure should reach to the top of the frames and lights, and after being trodden down, it should be well watered so as to accelerate the generation of heat.

Before placing the lights on the frames the soil should be watered if inclined to be dry, and even a layer of manure may be spread over the beds to hasten the growth of the Asparagus. Care, however, should be taken to remove this manure as soon as the tender shoots appear above the surface of the soil.

During the period of growth a temperature of 60° to 70° Fahr. should be maintained, but no air whatever is given. Watering is, however, attended to when necessary, as a humid atmosphere is essential to secure the best results.

Every ten days or a fortnight the frames should be banked up or " lined " with large or small quantities of fresh manure according to the state of the weather, the object being to maintain an even temperature within the frames.

Light is excluded during the daytime with mats ; and during the night-time the lights must also be covered with one or more mats according to the state of the weather. The temperature inside the frames should never fall below 55° Fahr., otherwise the shoots will be attacked with " rust " and become unsaleable.

Under these conditions fine shoots of Asparagus will be ready at the end of twenty to twenty-five days after forcing has commenced, and then cutting may take place every two or three days until the crop is exhausted, which takes place in from four to six weeks. After each cutting it is a good plan to stand the shoots in clean water, and place them in a cellar for a short time so that the tips may become tinged with colour.

When the crop is finished, the beds and linings of manure may be left untouched for several days to allow the heat to subside gradually, and also so that the plants may not be exposed too suddenly from a high to a low temperature. The frames and lights are then taken off, the manure from the pathways is utilised for dressing the ground for other vegetables, and the upper soil from the beds is returned to the pathways from which 'it was originally taken.

In practice, it is found more economical to force two beds of Asparagus running parallel than one, as the hot manure in the pathway then serves to heat both beds at the same time, and also to supply moisture by capillary attraction. To secure a succession of produce to the end of the season, an interval of from four to six weeks may be allowed between each bed, or group of beds, to be forced.

As a rule only half the beds are forced one year, so that the other half shall have a rest, thus allowing the plants to recover from the strain placed upon them by the forcing process.

Summer Treatment.—During the summer months the plants that have been forced are allowed to grow naturally without further picking, while those that are to be forced the following year are also allowed to grow naturally and without being cut.

Treated in this way Asparagus beds made in the way described will continue to yield good crops for twelve to fifteen years of what is known as " white " or " blanched " Asparagus.

Green Asparagus.—The plants used for the production of " green " Asparagus should be at least two, if not three, years old, to secure the best results.

These may be raised from seeds and transplanted in the way already described at p. 72, remembering that a good annual top-dressing of manure in the autumn or early winter months is necessary. A few good soakings during dry seasons are also advisable, and care should be taken to have the tall stems staked up before they begin to lie upon the ground.

When raising plants in this way for forcing later on, no young shoots whatever must be cut from them, as it is essential to develop strong, sturdy crowns with as many growths as possible. Of course each autumn the flowering stems are cut down to the ground, except the last year, when the crowns are to be forced. Then it is better to leave a few inches of the stems showing well above the soil to indicate the exact position of the plants, and to render the lifting as easy as possible.

Forcing " Green " Asparagus.—Forcing is practised from the middle of September till the beginning of March. The clumps or crowns are carefully lifted with a flat-tined fork, and are placed side by side on a few inches of rich mould that has previously been spread over the prepared hot-bed, or in a heated frame or warm greenhouse.

Each season large growers of Asparagus advertise two or three year-old crowns, for forcing purposes, at reasonable rates, so there is really no necessity for the intensive cultivator to devote time, labour, and land to the development of the plants.

When a bed is used for forcing, it is made up of good manure until it is 2 to 3 ft. thick, and developing a temperature of 70° to 80° Fahr. An excellent hot-bed may be made from equal parts of fresh stable manure, old manure, and cow manure—all of which should be well mixed together, and watered if inclined to be dry.

The frames are placed on the beds when ready, and the pathways between are filled half-way up with manure. On the surface of each bed 2 to 3 in. of mould is spread, so that the roots of the Asparagus shall not come in direct contact with the manure, and so that their growth shall be hastened without running the risk of being burned.

When the heat of the bed has sunk to 70° or 80° Fahr., the Asparagus crowns are placed side by side without having the roots shortened or mutilated in any way. The larger and taller clumps are placed near the top of the frame, and the smallest towards the bottom, and from 500 to 600 crowns can be packed in under each light, according to their size. When arranging the clumps it is important that the tops should be at the same distance from the glass, sloping gradually from top to bottom with the fall of the lights. Some fine rich and gritty mould is then carefully worked in between the crowns, and washed down amongst the roots with plenty of water ; after which some of the same mould should be spread over the tops of the crowns to a depth of a few inches.

Lining.—The work in the frames being finished, the pathways are then filled with manure up to the top of the frames if there is an inclination for the heat within to diminish. Manure is added or taken away from the pathways according as to whether the temperature is too low or too high. Towards night one, two, or three mats, according to the weather, should be placed over the lights for protection and to keep the heat constant by night as well as by day.

As soon as the shoots begin to grow, a little air may be admitted during the day if the weather is favourable, and sprinklings with tepid water must be given from time to time. At the end of about a fortnight, the first shoots will be ready for cutting, and others will continue to appear for about eight or ten weeks, during which they are gathered every day or two, the crop from each light varying from 6,000 to 8,000 shoots. These, being exposed to the light, develop green colouring, differing in this way from the white Asparagus produced in darkness.

When the crowns cease to produce any more growths the beds may be dismantled, or they may be made up again if it is still worth while to force another crop the same season. Once the roots have been forced in this way to produce " Green " Asparagus, they should be taken up and thrown away, as they are practically useless afterwards.

Open-air Culture.—It may be useful to English readers if the French method of growing Asparagus in the open air is described. So long as the soil is light and rather chalky, deeply cultivated and well manured at the beginning, the difficulties in the way of securing good Asparagus are not insuperable. A piece of land well exposed towards the south, and free from trees and shrubs, may be regarded as the most suitable place for an Asparagus plantation. At the same time shelter from the north and east by walls, fences, or hedges is a great boon, as the wind from those quarters has a retarding if not chilling effect upon the young growths in spring.

Preparing and Planting the Beds.—Having selected the site, the soil is dug about 18 in. deep and a good dressing of manure is incorporated with it, so that it decays completely during the winter months.

In the spring—about February—the ground is marked out in beds, each one being a metre (39 in.) in width, except the first and last beds, which are only half the width of the others. The soil in the second, fourth, sixth, and the following even-numbered beds is then dug a good spit deep, and " ridged up," half of it being placed on the odd beds 1, 3, 5, 7, etc., on one side, and half on the other as shown in the diagram (fig. 17). The trenches marked A, B, C, etc.,

FIG. 17.—DIAGRAM SHOWING HOW ASPARAGUS TRENCHES ARE MADE.

thus formed are well manured and deeply dug. Three " drills," or shallow furrows, are then drawn from one end to the other, one being exactly in the centre, and the two others each about 8 or 9 in. from the sides. More modern growers, however, draw only two drills in each trench about 9 in. from each side, so that more space is given to the plants. The best one-year-old " crowns " are then planted in each row so as to be from 24 to 30 in. apart, the plants in one row being angled with those in the other.

At the spot where each crown is to be planted a small heap of soil, about 2 in. high, is raised with the hands, and on this the young Asparagus plant is placed, taking care at the time to spread the roots out radially from the central tuft. A small stake is placed to each clump, to mark its position, after which the crowns are carefully covered by hand with a couple of inches of rich gritty soil. Some of the soil from the ridges on each side (see fig. 17) is then spread over the trenches to a depth of 5 or 6 in.

Summer Treatment.—During the summer months it will be necessary to keep the weeds down between the rows by frequent and careful use of the hoe, and occasional soakings with water will also be beneficial during very dry weather. About the end of September or early in October, when the stems have begun to wither, they may be cut down almost level with the ground. The soil is then carefully scooped away from the crown of each plant so as to form a circular basin about 8 in. in diameter. A little heap of some rich gritty soil and well-decayed manure and night soil is then placed in the basin over each crown, to serve as a fresh supply of nourishment for the roots, and also to throw off cold and heavy rains during the winter months. When performing this operation the spots where any plants have failed should be marked with a stick so that fresh plants may take their place the following year.

The ridges between the beds (see fig. 17) may be utilised during the first season for the production of early Potatoes, Dwarf Beans, Lettuces, and other salads if necessary, but late-maturing crops should be avoided.

Second Year's Work.—At the end of March or early in April, all vacant places having been replanted, the surface of the beds is lightly pricked up with a flat-tined fork so as to bury the manure placed over the crowns in the autumn. At the same period the ridges between the Asparagus trenches are dug over and manured, and prepared for such crops as early Carrots, early Potatoes, Dwarf Beans, Lettuces, Onions, and even Cabbages.

About the end of April or early in May, a few inches of soil should be drawn up round each clump of Asparagus shoots. As these are now numerous, it is necessary to place a stake about a foot away from the base of each clump, inserting it obliquely at an angle of about 45°, so that when the shoots become long enough they may be readily secured to the stakes. This not only prevents them from being blown about by the wind, but also enables the thread-like leaves (botanically known as " cladodes ") to be more fully exposed to the sunshine under whose influence only they can assimilate carbonic nourishment from the atmosphere to be stored up in the subterranean crowns.

Hoeings and waterings are to be attended to as in the first year during the summer months. In the autumn the stems are again cut down within a few inches of the soil, the stakes are taken away, and a good dressing of rich soil and manure is spread over each plant after the old soil has been scraped away from the top of it in the way already described (*see* p. 80).

Third Year's Work.—About the middle of March an examination of the old stems sticking above the surface of the soil will enable one to see which are the stronger and which the weaker plants. A mound of rich soil about 6 or 8 in. high is then placed over those with the stoutest stems, as these indicate greatest strength. The weaker crowns, with more feeble stems, are not treated in this way, but are to be allowed

6

another year's growth before any shoots are gathered from them ; they are, however, staked and otherwise attended to as already described for the first and second years.

The stronger crowns over which the mounds of soil have been placed will each yield three or four fine shoots. When these are 1 or 2 in. through the mound of soil, and their tops have assumed a purplish tint, they are fit to be removed. This may be done with a special Asparagus knife, or perhaps better still, by inserting a finger behind the stalk required so that when bent forward it easily snaps off. In this way there is not the same danger of injuring the other shoots as there is when a knife is used. Shoots from these plants may be gathered as long as they appear until the middle of June, but not later. All cutting should cease at midsummer, so that the plants shall not become exhausted too much. Stakes should be placed to the plants as already described, but before doing so, the little mounds of soil placed over the clumps in March should be spread evenly over the beds. In the autumn, the stems are cut down again, the soil is carefully removed from the crowns to the ridges, and in November a thin layer of rich manure and a little gritty soil is placed over the plants.

During this third year of growth the ridges between the beds should be dug and manured in the spring and prepared for such crops as Early Potatoes, Carrots, Lettuces, Spinach, or Dwarf Beans, etc., as in previous years.

Fourth and Succeeding Years' Work.—This is precisely the same as already described for the first three years. It must be borne in mind, however, that there will be more crowns to cover with mounds of soil in spring of the fourth year than there were in the third ; and there will be still more crowns for cutting in the fifth and sixth years than in those preceding them—until every clump of Asparagus is in full bearing and thoroughly established.

Each year the stout shoots only should be gathered from the strongest plånts, the weakest shoots and plants being given another season of growth to enable them to gather more strength. And in any case no shoots should be gathered after the middle of June, as each plant must be allowed to develop a certain number of shoots to store up nourishment in the crowns before the autumn.

From the sixth year onwards, the mounds placed over the crowns in March may be a foot or a little more in height, and also wider at the base, to completely cover the clump or " stool " of the plant beneath. When the shoots have pushed their way a couple of inches through the mounds they will have become tipped with rose, violet, or purple, and are then ready for gathering—a process that may have to be repeated almost every day, according to the rapidity of the growth. After cutting has ceased, the mounds are levelled, and the plants are securely staked and tied in the way already described. In October the stems are to be cut down, leaving a few inches sticking out of the soil to indicate their position. Some of the old soil is taken away from the crowns, and a nice compost of manure and a little gritty soil is substituted for it. Once the plants are in full bearing, an extra special dressing of manure may be given about every third or fourth year, and plantations treated in the way described will produce thousands of shoots for fifteen to twenty years.

As the clumps, " stools," or crowns of Asparagus increase in diameter, the ridges between the beds gradually diminish in width each succeeding year, so that it becomes impossible sooner or later to cultivate other crops on them as during the first years of forming the plantation.

Argenteuil Asparagus.—Argenteuil — an ancient town about six miles north-west of Paris—has been famous for centuries for its Asparagus plantations, and in the twentieth century the industry is as active as ever, if not more so.   The methods of culture described in the preceding pages are followed pretty closely, but the Argenteuil growers have their own system, which, however, differs only in detail.

When starting an Asparagus plantation the site chosen is first of all given a liberal dressing of manure— about 24 tons to the acre—in the autumn months. In February or March drills or furrows about 4 in. deep are drawn from one end of the ground to the other, 3 ft. and often 4 ft. apart.   The soil is then drawn up on each side so as to form ridges.   Between these the Asparagus crowns are planted in March or April, 1 metre (39 in.) apart.   A circular basin, about a foot wide, is made, 4 or 5 in. deep, and in the centre of it a little mound of soil is raised with the hands.   The Asparagus plant is then placed on the top of the mound, the roots are spread out in all directions, after which the crown is covered with a few handfuls of rich soil and well-decayed manure —the latter often being night soil.   During the summer months, the staking of the plants, hoeing, and watering, and other operations already described, are carried on until the stems are cut down in the autumn (see p. 80). When the beds have been established six years they are in full bearing, but from the third year onwards a few of the best shoots are gathered each season from the " crowns " that have been specially moulded up for the purpose. When in full bearing, the beds produce shoots for six or eight weeks, and these are generally gathered early in the morning, as they then retain their freshness for a much longer period. From the sixth year onwards, it is necessary to give a good dressing of manure every other year, and with proper attention the beds may continue to yield good crops of Asparagus for twenty-five or even thirty years. Special attention, however, must be paid to the following cultural details :

1. The plants should be 3 ft. or 4 ft. apart at the beginning.

2. Manure every autumn until the sixth year ; afterwards every other year.

3. Earth up the crowns in spring (see p. 81).

4. Never gather the shoots after the middle of April.

5. Level the mound of soil over the crowns in July.

6. Expose the top roots to the air in October by drawing the soil away from them carefully with the hoe.

7. In spring, clean each clump or crown from old or dead shoots and stems.

8. Stake the plants every year (see p. 81).

6 *

9. Cut only in accordance with the size and vigour of the plant.

10. Always pick by hand instead of cutting with the Asparagus knife.

By intelligent attention to these details the Argenteuil growers have made themselves famous in the Asparagus world.

CUTTING ASPARAGUS.—When the shoots of Asparagus are sufficiently advanced in growth to be picked, some little care is necessary in detaching them from the parent rootstock hidden beneath the soil. The professional grower scorns to use any instrument except his fingers. Having scraped a little of the soil away, he inserts one or .two fingers carefully behind the required shoot, gently bends it forward, and in this way snaps it off without injury to the other shoots. Various knives are used, however. One kind has a long shank inserted in a wooden handle, while the cutting blade is curved like a small scythe, and has a saw-like edge. Flat-bladed and semi-circular bladed gouges are also used. Whatever instrument is used should be pushed carefully down amongst the shoots. A dexterous twist is then given with the wrist, by means of which the shoot is severed at the base, and is brought above the soil.

BUNCHING ASPARAGUS.—To make the Asparagus shoots into nice bundles as seen in the shops and markets, special frames, moulds, or " bunchers " are used, as shown in fig. 18. It is quite an art, making and tying the bundles. The shoots are first of all picked over, and all those too small or too thin for the mould are rejected, and afterwards made into bundles by themselves, and sold as " Sprue." The best shoots are again graded into firsts, seconds, and thirds. The " firsts " or best shoots are first of all placed in the frame so that they shall be on the outside of the bundle when tied. The next best shoots are added, and the smallest are placed in the centre. When the required number has been placed in the frame, the bundle is tied up firmly with two osier twigs. These are previously steeped in water to

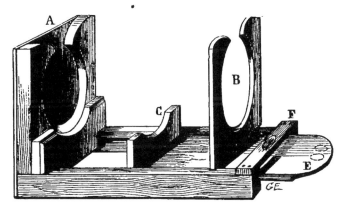

FIG. 18.—ASPARAGUS BUNCHER.

The board E, with fixtures B and C, moves backwards and forwards. The crosspiece F is for durability. The dotted circles near E indicate that there are two cavities underneath for the fingers to slide the board. When E is pushed back towards A, the Asparagus stems then rest on B and C, with the points towards A.

make them more pliable for the purpose. When complete, a bundle of Asparagus measures from 5 to 7 in. in diameter. Some growers, and probably the most sensible ones, do not mix thick and thin shoots in the same bundle, but make them up separately after having graded them. In any case, the neater the bundles are made, and the fresher and more equal in size the individual shoots in them, the more likely are they to realise a ready sale ; whilst badly made bundles consisting of irregular shoots are likely to leave the grower a sadder if not wiser man.

When one bears in mind that the best Asparagus fetches from 6s. to 15s. per bundle in market in the season, there is every incentive to select only the best shoots, and pack them carefully.

As the shoots do not retain their freshness beyond five or six days, they should be spread out on fresh-cut rye or other grass in a cool dark place free from draughts.

ASPARAGUS PESTS AND DISEASES.—The larvæ of the " Asparagus Beetle " (*Crioceris asparagi*) often do much mischief to young Asparagus plants.. The beetles lay their eggs on the stalks, and in due course the young maggots feed upon the more tender portions, doing great damage to the growth. The beetles themselves may be picked off by hand, or knocked from the stems by tapping with a stick, so that they are not allowed to lay their eggs. By syringing the plants once or twice a week from April to June with soft soap and quassia chip and nicotine solution, or any other well-known insecticide, they will be rendered distasteful to the pests, and these latter will be killed if they happen to be feeding at the time of spraying. Slugs and snails are also to be guarded against, as they eat the tender young shoots when pushing through the soil. They may be destroyed by dusting with lime and soot three or four mornings or evenings in succession and by keeping the beds cleared of any refuse in which they conceal themselves.

The " Asparagus rust " (*Puccinia Asparagi*), which sometimes attacks forced crowns when the temperature is irregular, rarely appears on properly grown open-air crops. As a preventive, the attacked shoots are detached and burnt ; and in the autumn when the stems have been cut down, but before removing the soil from the crowns, the beds are watered with a copper sulphate solution—about 1 lb. of sulphate of copper being used to 100 pints of water.

DWARF, FRENCH OR HARICOT BEANS

Although Haricot Beans (*Phaseolus vulgaris*) are not now grown so extensively, as a forced crop, by gardeners near Paris as they were formerly, it may be worth while describing the process. Being so easily grown in the open air during the summer months, it is obvious that unless a commercial gardener can produce his crops early in the year long before the open-air ones, he stands no chance whatever of being remunerated for his labour.

Although there are now many varieties of Dwarf Beans, those suitable for early or forced crops are somewhat restricted. Amongst the best for the purpose are : Early Dwarf Frame Haricot (*flageolet nain triomphe des châssis*), which grows 6 to 7 in. high, is very early, and has green seeds. As it is rather fastidious, care must be taken not to keep the seeds too moist when germinating. The Early Black Belgian Haricot (*H. noir hâtif de Belgique*) is a black-seeded variety, next in earliness to the first named, and a much stronger grower requiring more space. The Early Chalandray (*H. très-hâtif de Chalandray*) has yellow seeds ; the Early Dwarf Étampes (*H. flageolet très-hâtif d'Étampes*), a strong grower, with white seeds ; and *H. flageolet à feuilles cloquées* may also be grown. Formerly the Dwarf Dutch Haricot (*nain de Hollande*) was a popular kind for early forcing, but has been superseded largely by those mentioned. One variety with yellow seeds I think likely to succeed in England is known as " Six Weeks." I have grown it in the open air in the usual way, and much to my astonishment I picked the first pod exactly six weeks after the seeds were sown.

CULTURE.—About the middle of December a hot-bed varying from 12 to 24 in. in thickness is prepared, and on which a temperature of 65° to 70° Fahr. is maintained. A compost made up of two-thirds gritty loam and one-third old manure or leaf-soil is spread over the bed to a depth of 6 or 7 in. The seeds are then either sown where the plants are to develop, allowing sixteen or twenty-four plants to each light eventually; or they may be sown in pots or pans in a hot-bed or greenhouse, from which they are afterwards to be transplanted. This operation takes place as soon as the seed-leaves are well developed, and is considered to be an advantage, because the plants do not grow so tall and yield a larger supply of pods. Each young Bean plant is buried up to the seed-leaves in the soil; if this is inclined to dryness, a gentle watering must be given, and the lights must not be opened for a couple of days until growth has recommenced. Afterwards, air must be given on all fine days to keep the plants green and sturdy. Protection from frost is secured by covering with mats at night-time, the same being removed at the earliest moment each morning. In the event of severe weather, the frames must be banked up or "lined" with manure, more or less fresh, to maintain the requisite temperature within.

When the plants touch the glass they may be bent gently towards the top of the frame, and kept in that position by thin bamboo or other sticks placed across them. Apart from this, the frames may also be raised a little on pots or bricks, taking care, however, that the linings are made up well to prevent the cold outside air from entering at the base.

By this method of cultivation—somewhat costly and tedious apparently—the first pods may be picked six, eight, or ten weeks after the seed has been sown. As the season advances, succession crops will appear more quickly. The pods should be picked regularly and systematically before they get too old, as this is the only way to induce the plants to continue to yield for a long time. After March it is not worth while growing Dwarf Beans on hot-beds in this way, as the crops for the open air are being prepared.

Both "dwarf" and "runner" Beans have long been grown in greenhouses in England during the earlier months of the year—the plants being either in pots, or placed in beds. A temperature of 65° to 75° Fahr. must be maintained, and care must be taken to keep the atmosphere just in the right state of humidity—not too saturated on the one hand, or too dry on the other.

CLOCHE CULTURE.—Early crops in the open air may be secured by sowing seeds in gentle heat in April, afterwards transferring the plants to the open air when the seed-leaves are developed, placing three plants under every cloche. No air is given for a few days, to give the plants a fresh start, but afterwards as much as possible is given, until at length the cloches are taken off altogether when there is no longer any fear of frost. For good early Beans as much as 9*d.* and 1s. per lb. is often realised in market.

To have Dwarf Beans from October onwards, seeds may be sown in the open air on warm sunny borders. A sharp eye, however, must be kept on the early frosts in September and October. To guard against them, a light trellis of sticks should be made, and placed over the plants. At night-time, mats may be spread over the trellis to protect the plants from frost.

CABBAGES FOR SPRING

Nice Cabbages in the early spring are always highly appreciated, and when in market early are almost sure to command good prices. Amongst the best

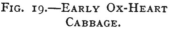

FIG. 19.—EARLY OX-HEART CABBAGE.   FIG. 20.—EXPRESS CABBAGE.

varieties for the purpose, mention may be made of the large and small forms of " Ox Heart," or *Cœur de Bœuf*, (fig. 19) and " Early York." There are several varieties of " Ox-Heart " Cabbages, one particularly early being called *Pomme de Paris*.

Other good sorts are " Express " (fig. 20), " Very Early Étampes " (fig. 21), and " St. Denis."

About the end of August, or early in September, seeds are sown, and these dates are very strictly adhered to. If sown much earlier or later the plants afterwards are inclined to run to seed instead of forming heads. About the end of September the young plants are ready for pricking out into beds, care being taken at the time to reject all blind, deformed, or diseased plants.

FIG. 21.—EARLY ÉTAMPES CABBAGE.

During November, sometimes even at the end of October, the plants thus pricked out will be ready for final planting. The ground is deeply dug, well manured, and levelled in advance, and the young plants have the stems buried until the lower leaves rest on the surface of the soil. They are spaced out 18 in. to 2 ft. apart in shallow furrows about a foot apart.

The soil in which the Cabbages are to mature should be deeply dug and well-manured, whether light or heavy in its nature. Parisian gardeners are particularly fond of night soil as a manure, especially for Cabbage crops ; but nearly all decayed vegetable refuse is also worked into the soil to enrich it in humus.

In the case of light soils, however, the sowing and final planting may be done a week or even a fortnight later than in the case of soils that are naturally inclined to be heavy or chalky.

From the same batch of seedlings it is possible to arrange for two distinct crops. This is done by placing some of the plants on warm and sheltered borders that have been deeply dug and well manured, as already described. Furrows 4 to 5 in. deep are drawn, and into these the Cabbages are planted. The soil thus drawn up in little ridges on each side of the shallow furrow serves to protect the " collar " of the young plant during the winter months. In the course of time the soil from the ridges gradually crumbles down, and, coming in contact with the plants, keeps them warmer than would otherwise be the case with plants on a perfectly level piece of ground.

The distance between the rows for winter planting

varies according to the nature of the soil and the growth of the varieties planted. For the " York " Cabbages and " Early Express " varieties, the rows may be about 12 in. apart. In these the

FIG. 22.—PARIS MARKET OX-HEART CABBAGE.

plants should be 15 to 18 in. apart. For the larger-growing varieties, however, such as the " Large Ox Heart," " Large York," " St. Denis," and " Market Ox Heart " (*moyen de la Halle*) (fig. 22), the rows may be 16 or 18 in. apart and the plants in them 16 to 20 in. asunder.

Planting, of course, is done in mild weather, many growers preferring to use the trowel for the purpose instead of the dibber. If possible a good watering is also given after planting to settle the soil nicely round the roots of each plant.

In cold or bleak localities the soil on the south side of the rows is drawn up carefully to the lower leaves of the plants, thus making a protecting bank so that the plants shall not suffer from quick thawings after a severe frost, or from the effects of a fall of snow. Some growers even go to the trouble during very severe frosts to cover their Cabbages with litter, or the straw from a manure heap, bracken, or anything else that is light and handy. Short dry manure may also be worked in between the rows, as still further protection against severe frosts and subsequent thawings.

During the spring months the plants are hoed well, and at the same time the mould is drawn up carefully about the stems. This not only serves as a protection for the plants, but it also helps them to resist strong winds and at the same time encourages the development of still more roots from the joints. From March onwards, if the weather is at all genial, a good watering now and then will be beneficial if the rains have not already made the soil sufficiently damp. When the plants are well-established, a little nitrate of soda—about 1 lb. to every 40 square yards—may be sprinkled over the soil, and afterwards worked in with the hoe.

Cabbages grown in the way described commence to turn in on the warm, sheltered borders during April and early in May, and are followed by the others grown in the open ground.

Some growers, when they see the earlier Cabbages beginning to heart, gently raise the large outer leaves upwards to the top, and tie them round the centre with a piece of raffia or rye grass. This makes the hearts eventually more tender and of a better flavour, while it accelerates hearting up. It is also an advantage to have the Cabbages thus tied up when one comes to pack them for market.

EARLY SUMMER CABBAGES.—For a supply of Cab-

FIG. 23.—FLAT PARISIAN (PLAT DE PARIS) CABBAGE.

bages during the summer months an early variety called " *Plat de Paris* " (fig. 23) is much favoured. It is so short stemmed that the large, flat heads appear to sit on the ground. Seeds of this variety are sown under cloches or in a gentle hot-bed about the middle of February, and are afterwards pricked out in nice soil at the rate of 400 plants to a light, or 30 under a cloche, when the seed-leaves are well developed. A little air is given when they have recovered, to keep them sturdy. Early in April these young Cabbages will be ready for the open air, and may be planted by themselves or between rows of Lettuces that are to be cut in May. After the Lettuces are taken off, the soil is hoed well, and if inclined to be dry, a good soaking of water is given occasionally. These Cabbages are ready by the middle of June.

CARDOONS

The Cardoon (*Cynara Cardunculus*) is a perennial composite, native of Southern Europe. It grows from 4 to 6 ft. high or more, and has large pinnate leaves, grey-green on the upper surface and almost white beneath. In many varieties there is a yellow or brown spine, often over $\frac{1}{2}$ in. long, in the angle of each division of the leaves. The fleshy leaf-stalks, when blanched, form the eatable portion of the plant, as well as the thick, fleshy main roots.

In many French gardens the Cardoon is an important crop. There are several varieties grown, such as the " Prickly Tours," " Ivory-white," " Spanish," and " Artichoke-leaved " or " Puvis," etc. Of these the first-named—" Prickly Tours "—is most highly appreciated by the market-gardeners of Tours and Paris, notwithstanding the fact that it is more spiny than any other kind. It is, however, also the hardiest and keeps better than the others, although all are susceptible to frost.

Cardoons are always raised from seeds, never from suckers. These are usually sown out-of-doors in May, in holes or pockets filled with rich gritty mould—three or four seeds being placed in each pocket. Or seeds may be sown in the latter half of April on a hot-bed with a temperature of 65° to 70° Fahr. The seedlings

7

appear in about 10 days on the hot-bed, those in the open air taking from 15 to 18 days to germinate in May.

When the young plants in the hot-bed have developed their seed-leaves, they are potted up singly into small pots and plunged in the hot-bed again. They are lightly sprinkled and kept rather close for some time, and are generally ready for planting in the open air about the middle of May, or a little later according to the weather.

In the case of the plants raised in the open air, when the seedlings are well developed all but the best one in each little hole are destroyed.

Whether the plants are raised in hot-beds or in the open air, it is essential to have them in rows at least 4 ft., but if possible 5 ft. apart. In all cases the young plants are placed in holes or trenches about a foot deep. The soil should be deeply dug and heavily manured in advance, the finest leaves being obtained on a sandy or chalky clay.

As the plants grow slowly at first the space between them may be utilised for raising such quick crops as Radishes, Carrots, Lettuces, Dwarf Beans, Spinach, early Cabbages, etc. The soil in the meantime is kept perfectly clean with the frequent use of the hoe, while the Cardoons are supplied with an abundance of water during the summer months.

BLANCHING.—This is essential. The leaf-stalks are tied up in two or three places according to length, in the same way as Celery, bearing in mind that the fierce and sharp spines on the leaves are capable of causing some trouble. To avoid being pricked with the spines, a strong stake, with a piece of stout string attached, is driven into the ground near the plant. The string is then wound round and round the plant, pulling the spiny leaves together into a bundle; or, " three sticks are used, one of them short, and connected with the other two by strong twine. The workman, standing at a safe distance, pushes the two handles under the plant, and then going to the other side and seizing them, soon gathers up the prickly leaves. Another workman then ties it up in three places, and straw is placed round and tied so as quite to exclude the light. In three weeks the vegetable is as well blanched and as tender as could be desired. To blanch the Cardoon properly and render the leaves perfectly tender, it should be deprived of light and air for at least three weeks. It is then cut just below the surface of the earth, and divested of its straw covering; the withered leaves are sliced off and the root trimmed up neatly " (Robinson).

This work is done during October. If it is desired to preserve Cardoons, the stems are tied up as described, the entire plant is taken up carefully with a ball of soil round the roots, and is plunged in well-decayed manure or leaf mould in a dark cellar free from frost.

CARROTS

The Carrot (*Daucus Carota*) is brought to great perfection in French gardens, and vast quantities of juicy, tender roots are grown year after year. The smaller-rooted varieties are preferred especially by intensive growers, as they are easily forced, are far superior to the larger kinds, and find a more ready sale not only in the central markets of Paris, but also in Covent Garden and other English markets.

The kinds chiefly grown are—

1. **Paris Forcing Carrot** (*syn.* "*Carotte rouge à forcer Parisienne*").—This is a comparatively new variety, considered to be somewhat earlier than the "French Forcing" or "Early Forcing Horn Carrot." The roots are somewhat similar in shape, but the skin is of a deep orange-red colour. It is highly recommended for forcing.

FIG. 24·—FRENCH FORCING OR EARLY FORCING HORN CARROT.

2. **The French Forcing or Early Forcing Horn Carrot** (*syns.* : "*Carotte très-courte à châssis*," "*C. grelot*," "*C. Toupie*," fig. 24).—This is the smallest and one of the earliest Carrots grown in hot-beds. The roots are almost round, $1\frac{1}{2}$ to 2 in. in diameter, suddenly narrowed into a long slender thread-like extremity. When forced in hot-beds the skin is generally pale or straw-yellow in colour ; but it assumes a scarlet tint when grown in the open air. The roots are very tender and of excellent flavour.

3. **Scarlet Horn Carrot or Dutch Horn Carrot** (*syns.* : "*Carotte rouge courte hâtive*," "*C. rouge courte d'Hollande*," "*C. Bellot*," fig. 25).—This excellent and tender variety is usually grown as a first-early crop in the open air. The roots are about 3 in. long,

and between 1 and 2 in. thick, the skin being deep scarlet, while the shape is cylindrical or long top-shaped, abruptly ending in a thread-like rootlet. It may be grown in hot-beds in the same way as French Forcing Carrot, but does not mature so quickly.

4. **Half-long Scarlet Carentan.**—This is an early

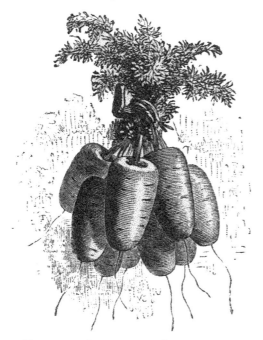

FIG. 25.—SCARLET OR DUTCH HORN CARROT.

FIG. 26.—SCARLET CARENTAN CARROT.

and finely coloured Carrot, excellent for later forced crops or for first crops in the open. The roots are narrowly cylindrical, suddenly ending in a thread-like tail (fig. 26).

5. **Half-long Nantes Scarlet Carrot** (*syns.*: "*Carotte rouge demi-longue nantaise*," "*Carotte sans cœur*").—This tender and fine-flavoured Carrot is good for early crops in the open air, but is scarcely profitable enough for forcing. The roots are bluntly cylindrical

7 *

in shape, 4 in. or so long, and between 1½ to 2 in. thick, with a deep red skin. It has very little core or heart, hence one of the French names, " *sans cœur* " (fig. 27).

There are many other varieties of Carrots, but as they are chiefly for open-air culture they need no special mention here.

FIG. 27.—HALF-LONG NANTES SCARLET CARROT.

FIRST CROPS.— Seeds of *Paris Forcing* or *Early Forcing Horn* are sown for the ˙first crop during October, on finely prepared mould about 6 in. deep on the surface of the mild hot-bed. After sowing the seeds and slightly covering them with soil, they should be gently beaten down with a piece of flat board. Very often, if not always indeed, Radishes are sown at the same time, but before the Carrots and a little deeper. Germination takes place in about a fortnight, and from this time onwards air is given on all occasions when the weather is favourable, if only for half an hour or so each day. This prevents etiolation or yellowing, and encourages the proper development of the leaves and roots.

In November, and again in December, sowings of the same varieties may be made on hot-beds about 18 in. thick, coated with fine mould to a depth of

6 in., and with a temperature ranging from 65° to 80° Fahr. At this period the seeds are sown rather thickly, about 3 oz. to 100 square yards. The mould covering the manure is mostly humus from old hot-beds ; it gives the skins of the Carrots a much brighter colour and a more tender flavour than can be obtained from ordinary garden soil.

Over Carrot seed Radishes may be also sown ; and from 30 to 36 Black Gotte Cabbage Lettuces may be planted over them in each light. These Lettuces will be fit to cut in January. As the Radishes develop quickly they are gathered before any damage is likely to be done either to the Carrots or the Lettuces—the latter of course being mature long before the Carrots—which will not be ready until early in April. A reference to the chapters on Cauliflowers, Radishes, Lettuces, etc., will show that Carrots are nearly always covered in the early stages with crops of a different character—usually just after the seed has been sown.

During growth attention must be given to watering, taking care that the beds are never allowed to become too dry. By keeping the manure in the pathways well moistened, there is no need to water the beds in the early stages, as sufficient moisture is absorbed by capillary attraction (see p. 15).

If the weather is very severe and frosty, hot manure must be placed between and around the frames to maintain the requisite temperature within. In mild weather, of course, less manure will be required between the frames than in cold weather.

Towards the end of March, if the weather is considered mild enough, the frames are taken off the Carrots and placed over other crops such as

Melons ; but then the Carrots will not mature quite so quickly.

During February and March, seeds of " Scarlet Horn " or " Half-long Nantes Scarlet " Carrots may be sown on open beds, without the protection of lights. Straw mats will afford sufficient protection from frost for these sowings. To keep the mats off the Carrots, two rails are fixed on stakes driven into the bed on each side. These Carrots succeed those from the earlier sowings, and fill in the gap between those sown in the open ground.

After the Carrots sown in February and March have been gathered, Radishes are sown on the same beds ; and when the Radishes have been pulled, their place may be taken with Celeriac (Turnip-rooted Celery) or some other crop.

THINNING CARROTS.—It is essential to thin out Carrots when they are 2 or 3 in. high, otherwise they would choke each other in time. The weakest seedlings are pulled up by hand, and about 3 in. of space is left between the first crops in frames, and one or two inches more between the out-door crops.

CAULIFLOWERS

The Cauliflower (*Brassica oleracea Botrytis cauli-flora*) is an important and often a lucrative crop to the intensive cultivator. Amongst the Cauliflowers proper (as distinguished from the hardier white-headed Broccoli) three sections are generally recognised, viz. the *tender*, the *half-hardy*, and the *hardy*—the varieties of which follow each other in natural succession. They may also be described as " early," " second early " or " mid-season," and " late." From the intensive cultivator's point of view the tender and half-hardy varieties are most valuable, as they come to maturity at a season when prices are generally high, and when the produce itself is most appreciated.

EARLY CROPS or " PRIMEURS."—Amongst the " tender " Cauliflowers the following varieties are considered best for " primeurs " or early crops, viz. :

1. E x p r e s s, considered t o b e t h e earliest Cauliflower of all, with short stems.

2. D w a r f E a r l y E r f u r t (*nain hâtif d'Erfurt*), a very early variety well suited for frame culture (fig. 28).

FIG. 28.—DWARF EARLY ERFURT CAULIFLOWER.

3. Early Paris (*tendre de Paris* or *Petit Salomon*), a good variety for spring crops.

4. Early Snowball (*Boule de neige*), one of the best for frames, especially in favoured localities.

SECOND EARLY CROPS.—The varieties of Cauliflower best suited to follow the above are—

1. Lenormand, short-stalked, a fine summer Cauliflower highly favoured by Parisian market-gardeners. It has a very short stem, large firm head of great purity, and keeps a long time (fig. 29).

2. Second Early Paris (*Demi-dur de Paris*, or *Gros Salomon*). This variety is highly esteemed for spring

and early summer crops, on account of its large beautiful white heads (fig. 30).

LATE OR OPEN-AIR CROPS.—There are several varieties adapted for this purpose, being characterised by their large leaves, sturdy stems, and large heads produced late in the summer or during autumn. Amongst the best-known kinds are—

1. **Autumn Giant**, with very large firm heads. If

FIG. 29.—LENORMAND CAULIFLOWER.

sown in February or March it comes into use in October and November.

2. **Walcheren**, a well-known variety with large white heads. It is very hardy and is best sown about April to produce heads in autumn and winter.

3. **Early London** or **Early Dutch**, a hardy variety much grown in Holland, but well adapted for English gardens. The heads are not particularly large, but they are hard and firm

CULTURE OF EARLY CAULIFLOWERS.—After the
1st and before September 20, seeds of early kinds
like " Express," " Dwarf Early Erfurt," " Early
Snowball " or " Early Paris " should be sown on an
old hot-bed, or even on open ground that has been
deeply dug and levelled, and afterwards covered with
a good layer of rich gritty mould. Seeds may also

FIG. 30.—SECOND EARLY PARIS (OR GROS SALOMON) CAULIFLOWER.

be sown at the same period, if the weather is unfavourable, under cloches or lights. In all cases the
seeds should be lightly covered with gritty soil, and
the seed-bed should be gently beaten down with the
back of the spade or a piece of flat board, afterwards
giving it a gentle watering through a fine-rosed can ;
and the seed-bed must be kept in a moist condition
afterwards—otherwise the germinating seeds may
suffer considerably.

When the seeds are sown under cloches or lights, air must be given more or less freely, according to the state of the weather, when the young plants are well through the soil. This will keep them strong and sturdy, otherwise they are apt to become weak and lanky.

Pricking out and Transplanting.—When the seedlings have made two leaves beyond the seed-leaves or cotyledons, they are ready for pricking out. This is done under lights or cloches, under which they are kept until ready for the final planting.

Some growers transfer the young Cauliflowers direct from the seed-bed to the ground on which the plants are to mature, and do not go to the trouble of moving them twice. But in this case they sow the seeds thinly, so that the young plants may not be too close, and may thus remain longer in the seed-bed if necessary.

Having marked out as much ground as is necessary, it is dug and prepared for the reception of the frames, which are to slope towards the south. The interior is filled up within 6 in. of the top with fine rich mould evenly spread over the surface and gently trodden down for the reception of the young plants. These should be well watered an hour or two previous to lifting, so as to have a good ball of soil to the roots. They are best taken up with a spade, great care being taken when separating the plants to retain as much soil as possible round the roots of each. The planting is done either with the finger or a small dibber, taking care to bury the young plants up to the seed-leaves, as this encourages adventitious roots to spring from the stems beneath the surface of the soil. About

3 to 4 in. space is left between each plant ; in other words, from 150 to 220 plants are placed under each light.

The planting finished, a nice sprinkling is given overhead, and the outside air is shut out for a few days until the plants pick up again. After this, air must be given on all fine days by tilting the lights with a piece of wood, brick, or flower-pot—whichever happens to be most convenient. •

Cloches.—When Cauliflowers are pricked out under cloches, raised sloping beds (see fig. 1) wide enough to accommodate three rows of glasses, are prepared and covered with fine rich mould. An impression of the cloches having been made on the surface by pressing down in the required spots, nineteen plants are usually placed under each one. The treatment is then the same as under lights.

It sometimes happens that the young plants under lights and cloches grow too quickly and would very soon stifle each other if not moved. Other beds for lights and cloches must then be prepared as in the first case. The plants are carefully taken up and transferred to these new quarters, but naturally at a greater distance from each other than before—so that each light holds only 80 to 140 plants, and each cloche about 14 instead of 19 as at first. This second pricking out retards the plants, and makes them generally hardier and more sturdy. It is also considered to make the plants mature earlier and to develop smaller " heads."

Protection.—From November onwards the young Cauliflower plants must be protected from severe frosts by means of mats spread over the frames or cloches at night. These, however, must be taken off as early as possible every morning, and air must be given freely on all genial days. In very severe weather, not only are mats used, but manure is also heaped round the frames, and leaves or litter are placed round the cloches.

When the temperature is so low that it is unsafe to take off the mats, or to give light and air to the plants, one must be careful not to uncover afterwards when the sun is too bright, nor yet to give too much air. It is better to avoid rapid changes in temperature, and to admit light and air carefully after a long period of darkness and a close atmosphere.

Final Planting of First Crop.—Early in December the hot-beds are made up, and a layer about 7 in. thick of rich sandy loam and leaf-mould, or old manure and sandy soil (three parts of manure to one of soil), is spread evenly over the surface.

Before taking the young plants from the beds or cloches in which they were pricked out, they should be well watered. They are then easily lifted, each one with a nice ball of soil attached to the roots. The plants should be carefully examined, so that only clean healthy ones shall be planted. " Blind " plants—that is, those in which the centre has been destroyed and has come malformed—and any that are too coarse in growth, besides those affected with disease at the base, are to be discarded. Six Cauliflowers are then planted under each light, three in a row at the top or north side, and three in a row at the bottom or south side. After planting, they are watered well and air is excluded for two or three days until they recover from the transplanting.

Afterwards air must be given on all favourable occasions and watering must be given more and more freely as the plants increase in vigour and approach maturity. Later on, as the leaves begin to touch the glass, if the weather is mild enough the frames and lights are taken away and placed over other crops. If, owing to the weather, it is risky to shift the frames, they may be lifted by placing blocks of wood or bricks beneath the legs at the corners. In this way more head room will be given the plants.

Early in March the heads begin to appear. To keep them perfectly white, as they increase in size one of the large leaves near the top is cracked at the base, and bent over the head. The exposure to light tends to make the heads yellowish in colour—a fact which lowers their market value.

The heads are fit to cut from about March 20 onwards and well into April, those which are just at the right stage being of course cut before the others.

Early in January another batch of young Cauliflowers from the same seed-bed may be planted; and still another batch a fortnight later, in beds on which Carrots and Radishes have been sown, and upon which Cos and Cabbage Lettuces are growing. Under favourable conditions "heads" are often fit to cut about the end of April and during May.

Intercropping.—In December when the young Cauliflowers—six in each light—are planted, there is much vacant space. This is often utilised for other crops, such as Cabbage Lettuces and Radishes. Seeds of the latter are sown and covered, and afterwards three rows of Gotte Lettuce are planted between the two rows of Cauliflowers. As the temperature of the frames at this period should be between 65° and 75° Fahr., the Radishes germinate quickly and mature long before they interfere with the Lettuces. The latter also, being quicker in growth than the Cauliflowers, will be fit to cut before the Cauliflowers will require more space.

SPRING AND SUMMER CAULIFLOWERS.—In the first half of September seeds of a variety like " Lenormand " or " Second Early Paris " (Gros *Salomon*) may be sown in the same way as the first crops.   When the young plants have developed two leaves beyond the seed-leaves, they are pricked out under lights, and grown on until large enough for the final transplanting in due course. This may take place in frames specially set apart for Cauliflowers, in which case Lettuces may be planted between, after another sowing of Radishes has been made in the way already mentioned.   Or the young Cauliflowers may be planted amongst the Carrots in other frames, placing three plants on the north side and three on the south side in each frame—with the Carrots in the centre.

Cauliflowers may also be planted in the spaces between the cloches that are sheltering Cos and Cabbage Lettuces, as shown at p. 153 in the diagram (fig. 41).

Between the beginning of February and the middle of March, other batches of Cauliflowers from the autumn sowings may be planted on warm sunny beds or borders, upon which Carrots and Radishes have previously been sown.   The Cauliflowers should be placed about 2½ ft. apart in rows 3 ft. apart, and should be " angled "—that is, so as not to be opposite each other in the rows.   At the same time a Cos

(Romaine) Lettuce may be planted between each Cauliflower, and Cos Lettuces may also be planted between the rows. The margins of the beds or borders may then be planted with Cabbage Lettuces as shown in the annexed diagram, in which a * represents Cauliflowers, an o Cos Lettuces, and an x Cabbage Lettuces.

x	x	x	·	x	x	x	x
*	o	*	o		*	o	*
o	o	o	o		o	o	o
o	*	o	*		o	*	o
x	x	x	x		x	x	x

SUCCESSION CROPS.—Seeds of the second-season varieties may be sown in February and March under similar conditions, or seedlings from the September sowing may be held over somewhat later than those that are to produce the second crop. The plants will be ready for planting in their final quarters in March or in April, when there is no longer need for artificial heat. Old beds may be used for these crops, or the young Cauliflowers (which should have been gradually hardened off in the frames) may be planted out on the warm, sheltered borders on which Cos and Cabbage Lettuces may have been already planted some time previously. These Cauliflowers will be ready at the end of May and during June and July.

If another sowing is made about the end of April or early in May of the same varieties—" Lenormand " and " Second Early Paris " (Gros Salomon)—the young plants will be ready for the open ground early in June. The soil in which they are placed, about 2 ft. apart every

8

way, should have been deeply dug and well enriched with manure in advance, if it is not already an old hot-bed. The plants must be kept watered well, and during August and September ought to yield fine heads. When first planted out in June, the ground between the Cauliflowers may be utilised for Cos or Cabbage Lettuces.

LATE CAULIFLOWERS.—To secure the latest Cauliflowers, seeds of " Autumn Giant," " Walcheren," or " Early London " may be sown at intervals from February and March to May or June in an old hot-bed or on a somewhat sheltered border. The last of the young plants, after pricking out in the usual way—or even transferring direct from the seed-bed—will be ready for final planting about July. They must be constantly watered to keep them growing steadily with soft and tender tissues. According to the period of sowing and the variety, the heads will come into use from August to October and November.

Late Cauliflowers may be intercropped much in the same way as those preceding them. Fine- and broad-leaved Endives, Radishes, Spinach, or Corn Salad are recommended as suitable for the purpose.

Covering the Heads.—This is essential in open-air crops. When the heads are forming up nicely, one or two large healthy leaves may be cracked low down, and then bent over them to protect them from the sun. These coverings should be examined each day in case caterpillars attack the heads, and in showery weather a watch must be kept for slugs. Indeed, from start to finish Cauliflowers are beset by many insect foes, one of the worst being the Turnip Beetle (*Haltica nemorum*). By frequently watering the plants, however, it may be kept in check. During early growth, if the plants are syringed occasionally with a little weak paraffin emulsion, the foliage will be rendered noxious to the various pests. About an egg-cupful of paraffin to three or four gallons of warm water, well mixed up with a little soft soap, will make a good solution. It should be applied in a fine spray morning or evening.

CELERY

The Celery (*Apium graveolens*) is a native biennial plant that has become of great garden value by selection and cultivation for centuries, and as a salad the leaf-stalks are highly esteemed. For intensive cultivation French gardeners favour a variety called " *Chemin* " or " *Plein blanc doré*," and known to us as " Paris Golden." This has leaves and stems of a golden-yellow colour, and matures quickly. It is, however, somewhat susceptible to frosts, and therefore is more valued for early crops. Other forms of this Celery are known as " *Plein blanc d'Amérique*," or " White Plume," and " *Plein blanc à côtes roses*," or " Pink Plume," both of which are also much grown in France for early crops, owing to the fact that the stems blanch readily without being " earthed up " very much.

From the end of January until about the middle of March seeds of the varieties mentioned may be sown on hot-beds having a temperature of 60° to 70° Fahr. To encourage rapid germination, frequent sprinklings are given, and when the young plants appear as much air as possible is given in accordance with the state of the weather, so that the plants may become sturdy. If the seedlings (from seeds sown in January) are too close together, they may be either " thinned out " or " pricked out," 3 to 4 in. apart, on an old hot-bed, when four or five leaves have developed. Seedlings from later growings in February and March may be pricked out when large enough in cold frames, under cloches, or even on warm south borders.

In April, when the earlier crops of Turnips, Carrots, Radishes, etc., have been taken from the frames, the young Celery plants may take their places. They will then be about 5 or 6 in. high. The plants are placed opposite each other, and not " angled," about 1 ft. apart in rows a similar distance from each other. After planting, the soil should be well watered to settle it about the roots, and a little litter or dry manure may be spread over the surface of a soil likely to dry rapidly. During growth attention must be paid to weeding and hoeing, and plenty of water must be given as the weather becomes warmer and growth more vigorous. As soon as the plants are about 18 in. high, they are ready for " blanching." If, however, the stems are more or less spreading, they should be tied together in one or two places, taking care, however, not to tie the tops too tightly, or the centres may be crippled and prevented from developing further. Plants from the earlier sowings will be ready for cutting about the end of July and during August ; while later sowings in April and May will produce plants for succession in autumn and winter. The green-stemmed varieties of Celery (*verts*) are best for winter use, owing to their hardiness ; while the *blonds* (sown in May) are recommended for autumn use, as they are easily blanched simply by spreading mats over them when nearly fully developed.

Blanching Celery.—This operation has the effect of excluding the light from the stems, which are thus rendered sweeter and more tender by the absence or non-development of the green colouring matter called chlorophyll. Different methods of blanching are adopted, but as the main object is the same in all cases, they differ only in details.

To blanch the earliest crops of Celery, dry leaves, straw, moss, or clean litter is placed between the plants where they are growing. A slender, wooden frame is slid in between the rows of Celery first of all so as to keep the leaves up and close together. The light-excluding material is worked in between the rows until about two-thirds of the stems are hidden. The frame is then withdrawn and placed between other rows that are to be treated in a similar manner. About fifteen days after this operation the Celery stems will be sufficiently blanched ; in addition, mats are often thrown over the tops of the plants at the same time to hasten the process.

Some growers, instead of placing straw or litter between the rows in the way described, make bands of the straw and then twist them round the Celery stalks from the base upwards for two-thirds of their length. This is an economical but less expeditious method of blanching. Other growers, again, use a kind of earthenware pipe 15 to 16 in. long, and about 6 in. wide at the base, tapering to about 4 in. at the top. The Celery stems are brought together by twisting a piece of string round them spirally from the bottom upwards ; a pipe is then placed over

8 *

each plant tied up thus, and the string is carefully unwound by pulling it through the upper hole in the pipe.

Another method of blanching Celery is adopted for the second or autumn crops as follows. A trench, 3 or 4 ft. wide, is dug out 12 to 15 in. deep, and of any required length, the soil being thrown up on both sides of the trench. The bottom is then broken up to ensure better drainage. The Celery plants are taken up, each with a ball of soil adhering to the roots. Each plant is " picked over "—that is, any dead or yellow leaves or basal suckers are detached, and the stems are fastened with one or two raffia or rye-grass ties, to prevent the soil getting into the crowns or hearts of the plants. The latter are then planted in the trench about 6 in. apart, in rows 8 to 10 in. wide, the ball of soil being just covered over. After planting, a good watering is given to settle the soil, and if the weather is dry the watering is renewed a few times so as to encourage the plants to become established quickly in their new quarters, which generally takes a week or ten days according to cir-cumstances.

The blanching, or "earthing up," is then done either in one operation or in two. If the former, the Celery stems are certainly whiter but not so firm and crisp as when the work is done on two separate oc-casions ; and the latter is recommended. The finely prepared soil is worked in between the rows of plants in the trenches, and the operation is facilitated by using a frame to hold the leaves up as described for blanching the early crops. About 6 in. of soil is worked in between the plants on the first occasion, and about a fortnight afterwards the operation is again performed. This time, however, the space between the rows is filled up with soil so that the stems are completely buried except for the leaves at the top. These stick out 5 or 6 in. above the soil, and as long as growth continues they carry on the work of assimilation. When danger from frost is feared the plants are covered with straw or litter, or mats, for protection at night, taking care, however, to uncover them as early as possible in the morning. About three or four weeks after the final earthing up the Celery will be fit for use, and will keep in good condition in the trenches until the end of February.

A third method of blanching Celery where it is grown is practised in the neighbourhoods of Meaux and Viroflay. Celery is planted in every other bed, and in the intervening spaces crops of Lettuces, Endive, Chicory, or some other vegetable are grown during the summer months. They must, however, be taken off the ground by September, as the soil on which they have been growing will then be required to " earth up " the Celery on each side. The work is best done on two occasions, with an interval of about a fortnight between ; the stems are then firmer and of a better flavour than if earthed up completely at one operation.

The English method of growing Celery is also adopted in some places. Trenches about a yard wide and 6 to 12 in. deep are prepared. In May or June two rows of Celery are planted in each trench. In due course the plants are " earthed up " by having the soil from the sides of the trench brought up to the stems in the course of two or three different operations. If necessary the stems are tied up, and any dead or yellow leaves are picked off the plants before the work begins.

Diseases.—The worst disease of Celery is caused by the Celery Fly (*Tephritis Onopordinis*), the maggots of which enter the tissues of the leaves and destroy them, causing unsightly blotches. The best way to check the pest is to syringe the healthy young plants frequently with the paraffin emulsion wash mentioned above under Cauliflowers (see p. 115).

CELERIAC OR TURNIP-ROOTED CELERY

Celeriac (*Apium graveolens rapacea*) is known in French gardens as " *Celeri rave* " (fig. 31), and differs

from the ordinary Celery in having swollen stems: These are cut up into slices and used in salads, and for flavouring soups, etc. For early crops seeds are sown at the end of February or early in March. The young plants will be ready for pricking out in April, either on an old hot-bed

FIG. 31.—CELERIAC OR TURNIP-ROOTED CELERY.

or on a warm south border, allowing 3 or 4 in. between them every way. Three or four weeks later, the young Celeriacs may be pricked out again in similar situations, this time about 6 in. apart.

Final planting takes place about the end of May, in the open air or in open beds, the plants being 12 to 14 in. apart and " angled " (*i.e.* planted quincuncially) in the rows. Sometimes they are grown between Lettuces or Cauliflowers, but this is not advisable. A succession may be kept up by making a second sowing in May, and planting out in due course after the seedlings have been pricked out twice, as already mentioned.

During growth weeds should be kept down by the hoe, and when the plants are about half-grown copious waterings may be given, especially during dry seasons.

To hasten the swelling of the stem in autumn, the lower leaves are removed as soon as they begin to look yellowish. When mature, the swollen stems—freed from leaves and roots—may be stored in dry, airy cellars, etc., where they will be free from frost.

Celeriac is now becoming better known in England, and it deserves attention on the part of market growers.

CHICORY, BARBE DE CAPUCIN, AND WITLOOF

Under these names, plants of *Cichorium Intybus* are largely grown for salading. To raise the plants, seeds may be sown in shallow drills in the open air in March or April, and if the green leaves only are used for salads, the seedlings need not be thinned out. The leaves are cut off close to the ground several times during the year when required.

When " Barbe de Capucin " is wanted, seeds are sown in the same way and at the same time. The seedlings, however, are thinned out about 6 in. apart.

About October the long thick roots are taken up, and are placed in close dark cellars or frames, with a little soil over them. Market growers place the roots upright on a hot-bed side by side, after clearing off the old leaves. They are covered with about a foot of gritty soil. In about three weeks' time, long narrow leaves, 10 to 12 in. long, are produced in the dark,

and, being beautifully blanched, form an excellent salad. When leaves cease to develop, the roots are taken out, and replaced with fresh ones from time to time during the winter months. The soil is watered occasionally if inclined to be dry.

Another form of Chicory is that known as " Witloof " (*i.e.* white leaf) or " Brussels Chicory " (fig. 32). It has thicker roots, and larger and wider leaves than the Barbe de Capucin. The roots are lifted about the end of October, and onwards during the winter, in the way already described. The old leaves are taken off, and trimmed within 1½ in. of

FIG. 32.—WITLOOF OR BRUSSELS CHICORY.

the top of the root, and any side roots are also suppressed. The main roots are then shortened to 8 or 10 in. in length. A trench, about 18 in. deep and 4 ft. or more wide, is then made, and afterwards filled up with light, rich, gritty soil. In this the roots are planted, so that the crowns are about 8 or 10 in. below the surface. To secure quick growth, about 1 ft. of hot manure is then spread over the bed, and about a month afterwards beautiful pale yellowish heads of excellent flavour are produced. The heads are gathered before the tips reach the manure—when within 1 in. or so from it, in fact—otherwise they would become discoloured and spoiled. A little raffia may be tied round the tops to keep the blanched leaves together. Witloof is eaten in a raw or cooked state.

CORN SALAD OR LAMB'S LETTUCE

This native annual (*Valerianella olitoria*) is becoming more and more highly esteemed as a salad in England each year, but it has long been common in France.

FIG. 33.—ROUND-LEAVED CORN SALAD.

The Round-leaved variety ("*Ronde*") is the one most highly favoured by the Parisian market-gardeners (fig. 33), but there are several others, perhaps the best being the large-leaved Italian Corn Salad, or Regence.

About the end of July or early in August seeds for the first crop are sown "broadcast," and then at intervals of three or four weeks until the end of October at the rate of about 3 or 4 oz. to 120 square yards. Before sowing, of course, the ground is lightly dug, trodden down again, and nicely levelled. After the seeds are sown, the surface is raked over, and some growers also add a light sprinkling of finely sifted mould. If the weather is very dry, a good watering will hasten germination, and is indeed essential to avoid failure altogether.

Many growers sow seeds of Chervil or Radishes at the same time as the Corn Salad, as one does not interfere with the other. Others, again, sow Corn Salad among such crops as Chicory, Endive, Cauliflowers, and Cabbages.

By sowing the Italian Corn Salad, or Regence, in October, either by itself or with the Round-leaved, a good succession will be kept up during the winter months, if mild.

CUCUMBERS

The long-fruited green Cucumbers (*Cucumis sativus*), as seen in England, are cultivated also by the Parisian market-gardeners, and much in the same way as in our glass-houses. In addition to these, however, " White " Cucumbers and small Prickly Cucumbers, or " Cornichons," are more or less extensively grown.

The first early crops of long-fruited Cucumbers can only be brought to perfection under glass during the early months of the year, and although they may realise a good price, it must not be forgotten that a great deal of the profit is eaten up by the high price of the coke or coal used in heating the boilers.

Frame Culture.—In the first half of February, and again a month later in the first half of March, Cucumber seeds may be sown on a gentle hot-bed, with a temperature of 60° to 65° Fahr., placing the seeds either in rows in the soil covering the bed, or in pots, or " pockets " (*i.e.* small holes made in the surface). A gentle watering is given, air is excluded, and mats are put on the lights at night for protection.

About ten or twelve days after sowing, when the seed leaves and first true leaves are well developed, the young Cucumber plants will be ready for moving into another bed with a similar temperature, allowing about 3 in. between each. The plants are sprinkled overhead, as before, with tepid water, no air is given for a few days, and shading is given from the sun. In a few days growth recommences, and the lights are tilted a little more and more each day, so that the air may harden the young plants and keep them sturdy. Towards evening, of course, " air is taken off "—that is, the lights are closed, and mats are spread over them in case of frost.

While the pricked-out plants are growing on, another hot-bed, 18 in. or 2 ft. thick, should be prepared for those that are fit for moving about the second week in March. From 6 to 8 in. of rich mould is spread over the surface of the bed, and when the rank steam has passed away, and the heat has subsided to about 70° or 65° Fahr., the bed will be ready for planting. Each little Cucumber is then carefully lifted, with a ball of soil adhering to the roots, and by means of a trowel, or even by hand, it is planted in the new frame up to the seed-leaves. Four Cucumbers are placed under each light, and when planting is finished tepid water is sprinkled over the plants before closing up the lights. No air is given for two or three days, so as to encourage the plants to " pick up " again quickly, and strong sunlight is also excluded for a few days for the same reason. Nor must covering up with mats at night be forgotten. Once growth has started, air is given on all fine days, and a sprinkling with tepid water is given in the morning and afternoon to encourage active growth.

When four or five leaves are borne on the main stem, the latter is pinched off 1 or 2 in. above the second leaf. This will cause two side branches to develop in due course. Before this takes place, however, a layer of straw or clean litter is spread over the surface of the bed. When the side branches are about 1 ft. long, these are also shortened back a little, in front of the second or third leaf. A third set of shoots will then commence to develop from these, and when they are about 1 ft. long, they must also be shortened back to the second or third leaf in the same way.

As soon as the young fruits have commenced to swell, the best and most shapely one is selected, and the shoot carrying it is pinched or shortened back to two leaves beyond the fruits. All others are suppressed. When this first fruit has grown about two-thirds of its natural size, a second fruit is chosen in the same way as the first, and when this attains two-thirds of its growth a third fruit is selected to keep up the succession ; and so on with other fruits, so that each plant may develop a dozen or more one after the other. All long shoots are then pinched back from time to time.

Watering, of course, must be attended to each day

if necessary, taking care to use water having the same temperature as that in the frame. If very cold water is used, the plants are likely to be chilled and stopped in growth. Air is given by " tilting " the frames on all fine days until the afternoon, when the lights should be closed to keep in the warmth during the night.

Cucumbers grown in this way, from seeds sown in February, are fit for cutting in April; in May and June from seeds sown a month or so later.

Cucumbers under Cloches.—Seeds may be sown in the first half of April in gentle hot-beds in the way already described, afterwards placing the young plants out in frames, and keeping them close and shaded for two or three days, until they start again into growth. Towards the end of April trenches and holes, each about 2 ft. wide, 1 ft. deep, and about $2\frac{1}{2}$ ft. apart, are made in a straight line on a warm sheltered border. These holes or trenches are filled with good manure to make a little hot-bed about 18 in. deep. The soil taken out is then spread over the heaps of manure in a layer about 8 in. thick, and a basin is made on top of each to accommodate a few handfuls of rich mould. When the rank heat has subsided, a young Cucumber plant is placed in the centre of each heap up to the seed-leaves, taking care beforehand to lift each plant with a nice ball of soil round the roots. The plants are watered well to settle the soil round them, after which each one is covered with a cloche, the upper two-thirds of which has been smeared with liquid whiting, lime, or clay, to serve as a shading against the sun. For three or four days the cloches are kept shut down on the soil, to encourage new growth. After this, however, the plants are ventilated on all fine days by raising the cloches—one, two, or three notches on the " tilts " in the way shown at p. 42. At night-time it may be necessary to cover the cloches with mats for protection against frost. When the plants have commenced to grow freely, the main shoot at first, and the others afterwards, must be pinched or shortened back in the same way as recommended for the plants grown under lights in frames, the only difference being that the shoots are left somewhat longer. The plants are watered well when necessary, and the cloches are taken off the plants altogether on fine days, replacing them towards evening. In due course the shoots will extend beyond the circumference of the cloches, and the latter may then be placed on three tilts to allow the shoots to spread naturally while protecting the main portion of the plant. As the weather is usually fine by the time the plants reach this stage, there is little danger from frosts, and the first fruits from Cucumbers grown in this way will be ready from the middle of June and onwards till the end of August.

Open-air Culture.—Cucumbers grown in the open air are generally raised from seeds sown in April in gentle hot-beds, afterwards transplanting in the way described about the end of May on little hot-beds for each plant. Seeds are often sown in such beds in May, and the plants from them are allowed to grow on without being disturbed. In the early stages it is wise to cover the plants with cloches until they are well established. While developing their growth, the vacant soil between the plants and along the margins of the beds may be utilised for a " catch crop " of Lettuces or Radishes. " White-fruited " Cucumbers, although practically unknown in British gardens, form a marketable crop in Paris. From inquiries made in the " Halles," as the Covent Garden of Paris is called, I was told that " White " Cucumbers were not grown anything like so extensively as the long green-fruited varieties—although the quantity grown found a ready sale. The fruits are somewhat similar in shape to the green ones, and at first are of the same colour. In the course of time, however, they pass from green to greenish-yellow, and ultimately to a kind of waxy or creamy white.

The raising, planting, and general cultivation is precisely the same as already described for the green varieties.

PRICKLY CUCUMBERS OR " CORNICHONS."—The small green Cucumbers chiefly used in pickles in England are extensively grown in the neighbourhood of Paris, and large quantities of them may be seen in the Paris markets during the summer months. These little Cucumbers must not be confounded with the small stunted fruits of the ordinary long green Cucumber. They are obtained from a special variety called " Cornichon vert petit de Paris." This is strong and hardy, and easily grown. The seeds are generally sown in gentle hot-beds early in May. In due course the young plants are pricked out in frames, and by the end of May or early in June they are again lifted with a nice ball of soil, and planted in little heaps of soil in the same way as Cucumbers. The shoots must be pinched to the third or fourth leaf, and when the branches are well developed a layer of straw or litter is placed on the soil for them to ramble over. The first fruits are ready by the middle or end of

July, and may be picked every two or three days until the crop is finished. The fruits are usually fit to gather about a week or ten days after the flowers have set well.

Insect Pests, etc.—Cucumbers grown in frames, under cloches, and in the open air are not so subject to attacks of insect pests and fungoid diseases as those grown in hot-houses. At the same time a watch must be kept at all times for slugs, who are very fond of them, and can only be kept in check by sprinkling a little lime and soot on the soil, and also by severing the bodies with a knife blade whenever they are seen. " Red spider " is a well-known Cucumber pest causing the under-surface of the leaves to assume a rusty appearance. As a dry atmosphere is the chief cause of " red spider," the natural remedy is to keep the surroundings fairly moist by watering and syringing as frequently as the growth of the plant and the weather necessitates. The " eel-worms " which are such a terrible pest in hot-houses, where they attack the roots of the Cucumbers, are not so prevalent in frames or the open air. When they appear, the plants are rendered useless and crops should not be grown in the same soil or in the same place a second time. The old soil also should be burned before using for other crops.

DANDELIONS

This well-known plant (*Taraxacum Dens-Leonis*) is usually treated with scant respect in the British Islands, although a few sensible market-gardeners are well aware of its value as a salad plant. The market-gardeners of Paris have paid attention to its cultivation for at least half a century, and it is now regarded as a regular garden crop by many—notwithstanding its abundance as a wild plant. Selection and cultivation have produced a better kind of Dandelion altogether, and plants are now to be obtained as large as small Cabbage Lettuces. Cultivation is simple. The seeds are sown in March and April, and the young plants are pricked out from May to August in rows, 12 to 15 in. apart, in a deep rich soil, the richer the better. During growth the hoe is frequently used, and plenty of water is given during dry seasons. The leaves may be picked during the autumn and winter months. If the roots are covered with a layer of soil in October, and forced in the same way as recommended for Barbe de Capucin (see p. 121), the Dandelion makes an excellent salad.

EGG-PLANTS OR AUBERGINES

The long violet-fruited Aubergine or Egg-plant (*Solanum Melongena*) is seen so regularly in the French and Belgian markets that it is astonishing the taste for this easily-grown fruit or vegetable has not yet spread to British gardens. The variety called *Violette de Tokio* is considered to be earlier than the ordinary kind. It is, moreover, dwarfer in habit and has larger fruits.

The plant is an annual, and is a native of India, and is also found in Africa and subtropical America.

To secure the first-early crops, seeds are sown about the end of November in the neighbourhood of Paris, on a hot-bed when the temperature is about 70° to 75° Fahr., covering them lightly with gritty mould.

No air is given for a week or so and the lights are covered with mats to accelerate germination. When this takes place, light must be admitted, and the mats are only put on at night for protection.

A month or six weeks after sowing, the young plants are pricked out on similar hot-beds, allowing 3 to 4 in. between each. A gentle watering is given. The lights are kept closed for a few days, and the young plants are shaded from the sunshine. As soon as signs of fresh growth appear, a little air is given in fine weather to keep the plants sturdy.

Where space, manure, and lights are available, Egg-plants may be pricked out a second time a fortnight or so after the first one, at least 6 in. being left between the plants on this occasion.

From eight to ten weeks after the seeds have been sown—that is to say, about the end of January, or early in February—the plants should be placed in their fruiting frames. The beds in these need not be quite so hot as those first made, as the temperature outside is gradually increasing each day. The bed is covered with about 8 in. of a compost half of which is sandy loam and half rich old manure. About six or nine plants are then carefully placed in each light, and a good watering completes the work. The lights are kept closed and the plants shaded for a few days, until they become re-established.

Intercropping.—The space between the Egg-plants need not be wasted. Seeds of " Gotte " or " George " Lettuces and Radishes may be sown between them, or young Lettuces of the varieties mentioned may be pricked out in the rows.

As soon as the Egg-plants have again started into

growth, air must be given on all favourable occasions, otherwise the plants will become " drawn " and weak.

When the main shoot carries two fertile flowers (not double or semi-double ones), the top may be pinched out. This results in the development in due course of four or five branches, each one of which is shortened back a little above the second flower. From ten to twelve fruits are thus secured on each plant, or from sixty to a hundred or more in each light. After the branches have been stopped in growth by pinching, all other side shoots are rigorously suppressed as they appear, so that the sap shall not be deflected from the swelling fruits.

The general cultural treatment consists in giving plenty of air on all mild days, to keep the plants as dwarf and sturdy as possible ; watering in the morning as required by the freedom of growth, and an occasional syringing with soapy water in the event of insect attacks. If any of the plants are too weak to stand alone, a stake must be placed to such, and the main stem and branches tied to it with raffia. In the event of the plants becoming too tall for the lights before it is safe to remove these altogether, extra height is secured by placing a second frame on top of the first.

The fruits from the first crop sown at the end of November generally ripen about five months after sowing the seeds, which brings the season to about the end of April or early in May.

A succession of fruits may be kept up by sowing seeds every month or six weeks according to requirements. With each succeeding crop less heat is required in the beds, and at the end of May onwards

9 *

the lights may be removed altogether if fine weather prevails.

It is doubtful if it would be worth the while of any British market-grower to devote space to the culture of Egg-plants, as even in France the prices realised of late years have declined a good deal.

ENDIVES

Endive (*Cichorium Endivia*), supposed to have come originally from India, is an excellent salad plant, and as such is extensively grown by French market-gardeners. Although treated as an annual, Endive is really a biennial, and may be divided into two distinct kinds—one having the leaves broad and entire, the other having the leaves finely cut into crisped and narrow segments. The broad-leaved Endives are known as " Scaroles " or " Escaroles " to French gardeners, while the varieties with finely cut and divided leaves are called "*Chicorées frisées.*" Of the latter there are many varieties, the best-known being the Italian, or " *Chicorée fine d'été,*" one of the quickest growing and much cultivated in frames. Others are the " Stag's Horn," or *Rouen, Picpus, Ruffec, Meaux* (Fine-curled Winter), *Passion,* and *Reine d'hiver* (Winter Queen), *La Parisienne* or Green Curled Paris (fig. 34)—all excellent varieties for growing in the open air, although the first-named (the *Rouen*) is grown in frames in spring.

Frame Culture.—Early in September, and again in October, seeds of the Italian Endive (*Chicorée fine d'été*) are sown under cloches, but not on hot-beds. When large enough to handle, the seedlings are pricked out—a dozen under each cloche. About the end of October or early in November plants are also pricked out into cold frames, giving as much air as possible after the first few days, so as to prevent the young plants rotting or " damping off." These plants will be fit to gather in January and February, and, if necessary, the frames which have been utilised for their culture then become available for forcing Asparagus (see p. 76).

FIG. 34.—GREEN CURLED PARIS ENDIVE (LA PARISIENNE).

Hot-bed Culture.—About the middle of October a hot-bed is made up, and when the heat has subsided until the temperature is about 75° to 85° Fahr., about 5 in. of gritty mould is spread over the surface—which should be not more than 2 or 3 in. away from the glass. The seeds are then sown, some growers afterwards covering them lightly with a little fine gritty mould, others contenting themselves by patting them down with a piece of board. In either case a gentle watering is given, the lights are put on the frames, and are covered with mats. This is to ensure rapid germination, which is necessary to prevent the plants running to seed afterwards, and takes place in about forty-eight hours or less, if the seeds are not too old. Once the young plants appear, the mats are put on at night and taken off as early as possible in the morning, and the lights are tilted a little to admit fresh air on all occasions when the weather is favourable.

Pricking out.—About ten or fifteen days after the seeds have been sown, the young plants will be ready for pricking out, either with the finger or a small stick. For this purpose another hot-bed, similar to the first, must have been prepared, the only difference being that the surface of the mould spread over the manure must be from 4 to 5 in. away from the glass. The young plants are spaced out 2 to 3 in. from each other all ways, and are buried up to the seed-leaves in the soil. The seedlings are gently watered with a fine-rosed waterpot, and after the lights are put on the frames they are not opened for two or three days, until the young plants have recovered. The mats, of course, are put on every night and taken off every day, and a little air is given to strengthen the plants on fine days.

Transplanting.—From two to three weeks—that is, about the middle of November—after the young Endives have been pricked out as above, they will be large enough for transplanting finally. This will be done on another prepared bed having a temperature of 70° to 80° Fahr. The manure in the hot-bed should be covered with a compost about 6 in. thick, made up of two-thirds leaf-soil or old manure and one-third gritty loam or good garden soil. The surface now should be about 5 or 6 in. from the glass, to allow the plants sufficient space to heart up. About three dozen plants are placed under each light, after which they are nicely watered and kept " close " for a few days, and also slightly shaded.

Once established, air is given on all fine days on the leeward side, and the plants are given water whenever they require it, judging by the condition of the soil,

Fig. 35.—Broad-leaved Batavian Endive.

etc. At night-time mats must be spread over the lights—sometimes two or three thick in very frosty weather. They should, however, be removed as early as possible in the morning.

In the event of the heat declining in the beds, it will also be necessary to " line " the frames with fresh manure.

About the end of January—that is about three months and a half from the date of sowing the seeds in mid-October—the Endives will be ready to gather.

Seeds of Endive may also be sown in the way described about the middle of January, to be ready by the middle of March; and again in the middle of February for gathering in May. As the season advances and becomes naturally warmer, it will not be necessary to make the hot-beds so thick or with so much fresh manure as for those used during the colder months of the year.

From the middle of March, fine-leaved Endives may be sown under cloches or in cold frames, pricking out the seedlings and transplanting in due course in the way already described. As the season advances, the lights or cloches may be taken off the plants altogether in fine weather. They must be kept growing steadily by giving plenty of water, almost every day it does not rain, otherwise there is a danger of the plants running to seed or " bolting."

Intercropping.—During the summer months Endives in the open air are intercropped with Cos and Cabbage Lettuces, and later on in the season Spinach or Corn Salad is often sown between the rows. I have seen such plantations in the neighbourhood of Vitry in August, and was astonished at the use made of every square inch of ground.

The broad-leaved or " Scarole " Endives possess a hardy constitution and are finely flavoured. The most popular varieties are the "Batavian" or "*Scarole ronde,*" " Green-market " or " *Verte maraîchère,*" chiefly grown for autumn and winter use; while the " *Scarole blonde,*" or " Lettuce-leaved Endive," is an early variety that comes into use in June and July from seeds sown about the middle of April on a bed having a temperature of 65° to 70° Fahr. The " *blonde* " Endives are planted about 1 ft. apart every way, but the "Batavian" (fig. 35) (" ronde ") or " *Verte maraîchère* " kinds

require another 2 in. Another large variety called
" *Scarole géante* " or " Giant Batavian," owing to its
size and vigour, requires about 18 in. between each
plant, to allow it to reach its proper size.

The autumn plantations should be made not later
than the first week in September as a rule ; and then
it would be wise to have the plants in beds of the
same width as the lights and frames generally in use,
as these are handy for protection if necessary.

Blanching and Tying.—There are many ways of
blanching Endives, but one of the simplest is to tie
the plants up in the same way as recommended for
Lettuces when they are sufficiently developed—say
when more than three-fourths of their growth has
been made. When the frosts appear, the plants
may be lifted carefully with a spade and transferred
to cellars or placed in frames—spreading some dry
litter or straw over the plants in the latter to exclude
the light. In the open air, after the plants are tied
up, they must be liberally watered when necessary,
to encourage the whitening " hearts " in the centre
to mature as rapidly as possible.

LEEKS

The Leek (*Allium Porrum*) constitutes an important
crop in French as well as in English market-gardens,
and it is probable that, so far as open-air culture is
concerned, there is but little difference in methods
employed on both sides of the Channel. Ideas,
however, differ a good deal, and the French prefer
the smaller and more quickly grown tender-stemmed

Leeks to the excessively large specimens seen in England.

The varieties selected for early crops by the Parisian gardeners are known as the " *Rouen*," the " Long Winter Paris " (*Long d'hiver de Paris*), the " Large Yellow Poitou " (*Gros Jaune du Poitou*), and the " *Gros Court* " or " *Été*," to which may be added the well-known "Lyon" and "Musselburgh" varieties. Whichever variety is chosen, the main object in view is to secure Leeks of medium size in the early days of June.

Seeds are sown thickly in the latter half of December on a hot-bed about 15 in. deep and with a temperature of 60° to 65° Fahr. To hasten germination, it is a good plan to soak the seeds in luke-warm water for about twelve hours—more or less—in advance. If the primary root in the seed begins to show, it may be taken for granted that the seeds have soaked long enough. They should then be sown at once, on a layer about 4 in. deep of rich gritty soil that has been spread over the manure in the beds, and lightly covered with gritty mould. Each day the soil should be sprinkled with tepid water until the plants are well above the surface. At this stage a little air may be given by tilting the lights on all fine days, but care must be taken not to subject the seedlings to cold draughts of air, as these cause a chill and consequent stagnation of growth. At night it will be found more or less necessary to spread a mat or two over the lights according to the weather, but such coverings must be taken off as early as possible the morning following.

This treatment is kept up with occasional waterings

until about the end of February or early in March. The young Leeks are then fit for pricking out into another fairly good hot-bed. Only the very best plants are selected, and these may have the roots and the leaves cut back in the same way as recommended for Spring Onions (see p. 186). A space of 3 or 4 in. is left between the little Leeks, and care is taken to bury them deeply—leaving only an inch or two showing above the surface, because deep planting means beautiful white stems later on. A good soaking is given, and no air is admitted for a few days until the plants have recovered. Afterwards air is given more or less freely on all favourable occasions, and the Leeks will be ready early in June.

From the same seed-bed Leeks may also be planted early in March on warm, sheltered borders in the open air, after cutting the roots and tops, and they will succeed those planted in the frames. They should be kept nicely watered in dry weather to keep the growth active.

Open-air Culture.—The soil for Leeks in the open air cannot be too rich and deep to secure the best results. Seeds may be sown at four different periods to keep up a succession, namely, (i) in February or March sow " Gros *Court* " or " *Jaune du Poitou* " to yield Leeks in August and September ; (ii) in April and May sow " *Rouen* " to yield from October onwards ; (iii) in July sow " Long Winter Paris " to yield at the end of winter and early spring ; and (iv) sow the same variety in the first half of September to yield in April and May and June the following year.

In all cases—except the September sowing—the seeds should be sown thickly, as the plants are thus kept very straight by crowding. When the stems are about as thick as an ordinary slate-pencil they should be lifted carefully, and the best selected for transplanting, after the roots and tops have been cut as described for Onions (see p. 186). The seeds sown in September should be sown thinly in drills, and as the weather is generally unfavourable, the Leeks are allowed to develop to the required size in the seed-beds.

An excellent way to secure nice Leeks from the earlier sowings is to select a piece of ground that has been deeply dug or trenched, and heavily manured the previous season. Drills about 2 in. deep and 1 ft. apart are drawn running north and south if possible. In these drills the best Leeks are planted deeply and 6 in. apart, after the tips of the roots and tops have been cut off. After planting, the soil is given a good watering, and when the Leeks are in full growth afterwards, attention must be given to watering when necessary. Indeed, weak liquid manure from the stables or cow-sheds, or made from guano and soot, etc., given two or three times a week will keep the plants in an active state of growth until they are required for use.

LETTUCES

As a salad, perhaps, there is no other plant equal in importance and popularity to the Lettuce (*Lactuca sativa*). It is quite as popular in the British Islands as on the Continent, and it is not too much to say that millions of plants are grown in market-gardens alone in England to meet the great demand there is for them—especially in hot seasons.

There are two distinct kinds of Lettuces grown, namely, (i) the " Cabbage Lettuce " (*Lactuca capitata*), and (ii) the " Cos " or " Romaine " Lettuce (*Lactuca sativa*). Each kind has several varieties, some being more suitable for frame and bell-glass culture, while others flourish in the open air.

They may be classified as follows for intensive cultivation :

I. CABBAGE LETTUCES

(*a*) EARLY OR " PRIMEUR " CABBAGE LETTUCES.— The seeds of the varieties belonging to this group are generally sown between September 1 and the end of February, and again in March for a succession on warm borders.

The varieties most in favour with Parisian growers are :

1. **The Crêpe** or **Petite noire Lettuce** (white and black-seeded varieties). Both kinds are grown extensively for the first-early crops, for which they are specially adapted, as they " heart up " without much air or water.

2. **Gotte Lettuce** (white and black-seeded varieties). The White-seeded Gotte (*syn.* Tennis Ball, Boston Market) is an excellent small-hearted frame Lettuce, but is not so early as the Black-seeded Gotte (*syn.* Paris Market Forcing). Good sub-varieties of the Gotte Lettuce are *Tom Thumb, Jaune d'Or* (*syn.* Golden Frame), the *George*, and another form of the Paris market forcing variety, *Gotte lente à monter* (or Black-seeded Tom Thumb).

(*b*) Second Early or Summer Cabbage Lettuces.
—1. **Blond d'été** or **Royale** (*syn.* White-seeded All-the-Year-Round). An excellent variety, nearly all " heart," small, but very prolific and early, and much grown.

2. **Palatine** (*syn.* Brown Genoa), a large-hearted, quick-growing variety, the leaves of which are washed with coppery red beneath.

3. **Grosse brune paresseuse** (*syn.* Black-seeded Giant Summer Lettuce or Mogul). A hardy and very

FIG. 36.—White Stone Cabbage Lettuce (Grosse blonde Paresseuse).

productive Lettuce, forming a high centre, tinged with brown (fig. 44).

4. **Grosse blonde paresseuse** (*syn.* White Stone or Nonpareil Cabbage Lettuce). An excellent summer Lettuce, with large tender long-standing heads (fig. 36).

5. **Blonde de Chavigny** (*syn.* Chavigny White-seeded Lettuce). A quick-hearting variety with pleasing yellowish-tinted green leaves.

6. **Merveille des Quatre Saisons** (*syn.* All the Year Round). An excellent Cabbage Lettuce for all seasons if a red-tinted variety is required.

To the above may be added the Brown or Red

Dutch Cabbage Lettuce (*Rousse de Hollande*), the Presbytery, Brown Champagne, and the White Batavian.

For "outdoor" crops in the British Islands, it may probably be safer, if not wiser at first, to rely upon standard varieties that have been well proved. At the same time the sensible grower will test several varieties in the hope of securing something better than he has already. •

(c) WINTER CABBAGE LETTUCES.—The varieties in this group naturally follow those produced in the summer and autumn, and are raised from seeds sown in August and September, to be grown on during the winter months with or without protection. The most popular varieties are :

1. **The Passion.** There are two varieties of this —the white-seeded and the black-seeded. The former (called "*blonde*") is recognised by the reddish tint of the foliage, while the black-seeded variety has pale green foliage without the reddish tint (see fig. 45).

2. **Grosse blonde d'hiver** (*syn*. Winter White Cabbage Lettuce) is a hardy variety, and produces its large tender hearts early.

3. **Morine** (*syn.* Hammersmith, or Hardy Green Winter Cabbage Lettuce). This is a small, but very hardy and productive Lettuce of good quality.

4. **Winter Trémont.**—A good and very hardy variety with large white hearts, the outer leaves, however, being tinted with rusty brown (see fig. 46).

CULTURE OF THE "CRÊPE" OR "PETITE NOIRE" LETTUCES.—The first sowing of these Lettuces takes place early in September, and may be made either on a warm sheltered border, a raised bed, or an old hot-bed protected by cloches or lights. When sown on a border the soil is first of all deeply dug and then levelled with the rake. The surface is covered over with a good inch or more of mould made up of old manure and gritty soil passed through a sieve.

The seeds are sown fairly thick, and lightly covered with the gritty mould, after which the seed-bed is gently patted down to bring the soil and seeds into closer contact. If inclined to be too dry, the seed-bed is gently watered to settle the soil and encourage germination.

When the seeds are to be sown under cloches, each little seed-bed is marked out by pressing down a cloche upon the prepared surface of the soil so that the imprint of its circumference is plainly seen. After sowing, the seeds are lightly covered with fine soil. The cloches are then placed over them, taking care to press the rims firmly into the soil to exclude air and to check evaporation. Germination at this period of the year usually takes place under the cloches in a few days. If the sun happens to be too ardent at the time, the cloches should be shaded with litter or mats, but no air is given. When, however, the young plants appear, shading must only be given when the sun becomes too hot, otherwise the plants become " drawn " and pale in colour.

Pricking out.—When the seed-leaves or cotyledons are well developed and the first true leaves begin to form, French gardeners prepare to prick out the young plants, either on a raised bed or " ados " (see p. 13), or under cloches or lights.

In the case of a raised bed this should be well exposed to the south if possible, and be higher at the back than at the front, the width being the regulation one of 4½ ft.

Three rows of cloches are placed on each raised bed. Under each cloche twenty-four or thirty Lettuces are pricked out (see figs. 37–8), the outer row being about 2 in. away from the rim of the glass so that the young plants may not be injured by frost. In the event of any becoming frosted they should be pulled out and thrown away, as they rarely heart up properly afterwards.

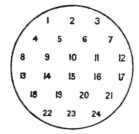

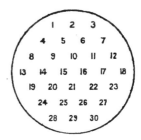

FIG. 37.—SHOWING HOW 24 SEED-
LINGS ARE TO BE PRICKED OUT
UNDER A CLOCHE.

FIG. 38.—SHOWING HOW 30 SEED-
LINGS ARE TO BE PRICKED OUT
UNDER A CLOCHE.

The young plants are usually pricked out with the finger, as there are fewer failures in this way than if a dibber or a pointed stick is used. It is also a quicker way of pricking out a large number of plants, and French gardeners are often whole days at a time on their knees at this particular work.

When the work is finished, the young plants are lightly sprinkled over with tepid water, and no air is given for a few days.

When frames are used, they are placed in a position sloping towards the south. They are filled up with mould to within 3 or 4 in. of the lights. A layer of fine sifted sandy mould about an inch thick is then spread over the soil, and the young plants are pricked out with the finger about $2\frac{1}{2}$ to 3 in. apart, after which they are gently watered, and kept " close," *i.e.* without air, for a few days until growth recommences.

Of course the little plants are carefully raised from the seed-bed so that as little injury as possible is done to the tender rootlets.

Shading.—Whether the young plants are under cloches or under lights, it is advisable during the first few days to shade them from strong sunshine. Once they have recovered a little air may be given to keep them sturdy. On the approach of early frosts the lights and cloches must be covered with mats during the night, and dry leaves and litter must be placed round the cloches.

First Crop of " Crêpe " Lettuces.—About the middle of October, or even earlier, the Lettuces that have been pricked out under cloches or in frames in the way described above will be ready for transplanting to their final quarters. Beds about $4\frac{1}{2}$ ft. wide are prepared by digging and levelling, but there is no need to use raised beds or " ados " at this period. Old beds from which other crops have been gathered are often used for this purpose, and as the plants require but little heat, the old manure and soil is simply turned over and made up afresh.

When cloches are used, three rows as usual are arranged, and under each one four plants of these " Crêpe" Lettuces are planted. In frames about 49 (in rows 7 by 7) or 56 (in rows 8 by 7) plants are placed under each light.

Each plant is lifted with a " ball " of soil round the roots, and any dead or decaying leaves at the base are carefully picked off. Care must also be taken not to place the " collar " of the plant too low in the soil, otherwise the lower leaves come in contact with the moist earth, and may be attacked by mildew.

After the plants are in position, a sprinkling of tepid water may be given to settle the soil round them, No air, however, is given to these early crops of " *Crêpe* " Lettuces, and once established it is even dangerous to give them water overhead. If the manure in the pathways is kept wet they will secure sufficient moisture by capillary attraction (see p. 15). Protection from frost by covering with mats at night and by placing dry manure or litter round the cloches or frames must also be attended to as required.

. This first crop of " *Crêpe* " Lettuces ought to be ready for sale by the beginning of December, or even by the end of November, according to the season.

The Lettuce plants are frequently examined and any decaying leaves are carefully removed to prevent the spread of mildew.

Second and Successive Crops of " Crêpe" Lettuces.— About every fortnight seeds may be sown to keep up a succession. Many growers, however, substitute the " George" Gotte Lettuce for the " *Crêpe* " for the sowings at the end of February and during March.

The sowings of " *Crêpe* " Lettuce made in October, November, and December are always made by themselves ; but those made at the end of December, January, February, and beginning of March may be intercropped with Cauliflowers. Besides, they are made on the same beds as the preceding, which will

10 *

have been re-made by adding about one-third of fresh manure to the old.

About the middle of February the old beds are sometimes re-made with a little fresh manure for the third crop. If, however the plants appear to stand still the frames must be " lined " or " banked up " with hot manure, no matter what the period of the year may be. Of course the mats are taken off the lights and cloches every morning as early as possible to admit light to the plants. It is well, however, before uncovering altogether to make sure that the plants have not been frosted. If they have, instead of taking off the mats, others are added so that the thawing may take place as slowly as possible. By this means injury to the plants is avoided.

In December, many growers, instead of making up special beds for Lettuces, plant the " Crêpe " variety on top of the Carrots which have been sown, and they are ready about fifty days afterwards—that is, some time in January.

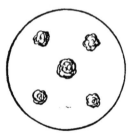

FIG. 39.—SHOWING HOW ONE COS (IN THE CENTRE) AND 4 CABBAGE LETTUCES ARE PLANTED UNDER A CLOCHE.

If the frost increases in severity, the frames are kept warm by filling the pathways with hot manure up to the top of the lights, and it may be necessary to have a double covering of mats during the night.

The last crop of " Crêpe " Lettuce is planted in January or February according to the weather. A hot-bed 12 to 14 in. thick is prepared. The surface is covered with a layer about 4 in. thick of nice gritty mould, and then the cloches are placed in position in three rows as usual.   Under each cloche four "*Crêpe*" Lettuces with one Cos (*Romaine*) in the centre are planted (see fig. 39).   During the night they are covered with mats as usual, and generally attended to, with the result that the plants are mature by the end of February or during March.

CULTURE OF " GOTTE " LETTUCE.—As already stated there are two varieties of " *Gotte* " Lettuce—the *black-seeded* or " Paris Market," and the *white-seeded* or " Tennis Ball." The latter is larger and later in hearting up than the former (fig. 40).

The general cultivation of "*Gotte*" Lettuces differs but little from that of the "*Crêpe*" or " *Petite noire*" varieties.   The first sowing may be made during the second half of October or during the early days of November, under cloches or on raised sloping beds.   The soil should be rather more sandy than for

FIG. 40.—WHITE " GOTTE " CABBAGE LETTUCE.

"*Crêpe*" Lettuces.   When large enough, the young plants are pricked out under cloches and on the raised beds.   Being larger in growth than the "*Crêpe*" varieties, only twenty-four plants of " *Gotte* " Lettuce should be placed under each cloche instead of thirty— the young plants being sprinkled and kept close for two or three days afterwards until they pick up again. Afterwards air is given more or less freely according to the weather, as " *Gotte* " Lettuces do not heart up well if kept too close.   Besides, it is not necessary to shut the cloches right down until two or three degrees of frost appear.   If, however, the weather remains cold and the frosts become severe, the plants must be protected by dry litter or mats.

About the end of January or early in February the " *Gotte* " Lettuces will be ready for planting under cloches or in frames, the soil and beds in which have been prepared for their reception in the meantime. The cloches having been arranged on beds—which should be at least 1 ft. thick, about 4½ ft. wide, and with about 4 in. of nice gritty mould on top— three " *Gotte* " Lettuces are planted under each glass, as shown in the diagram (fig. 47), without a Cos Lettuce in the centre, however.

In the frames, from which probably the " *Crêpe* " varieties have been gathered, and which have been re-made, 36 or 42 plants may be placed under each light. They are then gently watered in and air is excluded for three or four days to encourage root action and new growth. Afterwards air is given as freely as the weather will permit, until ready for market, which is generally about the end of March for those planted in January, and in April for those planted in February.

Intercropping.—Very often before the earlier crops of Lettuce are planted, Radishes are sown on the beds ; while with the later crops, Radishes and Carrots are also sown, although some prefer to inter-crop with Cauliflowers. As soon as the first crops have been gathered, the beds are re-made and prepared for those to follow them.

For the crops that are planted in March, many growers substitute cloches for frames, if Carrots have not been sown previously. Four Cabbage Lettuces and one Cos Lettuce in the centre are planted beneath each cloche. The spaces between the cloches are occupied by Cauliflowers as shown in the diagram. Before planting the Lettuces and covering with cloches, a sowing of Carrots may also be made. This method of cultivation enables one to secure four or five different crops from the same soil—Radishes, Cabbage Lettuces, Romaine or Cos Lettuces, Carrots, and Cauliflowers.

CULTIVATION OF THE " GEORGE " LETTUCE.—Just

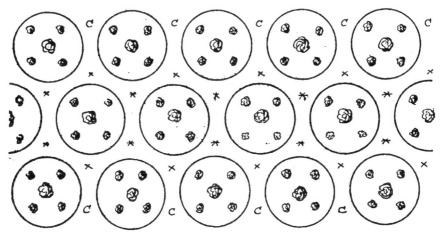

FIG. 41.—SHOWING 4 CABBAGE LETTUCES AND
1 COS LETTUCE BENEATH CLOCHES.
Cauliflowers (c) may be planted on the borders, and other later crop Lettuces at x and * to be covered in turn with the glasses.

as the " Gotte " Lettuces naturally succeed the "Crêpe" or " Petite noire " varieties, they are themselves succeeded by the " George " Lettuce at the end of February or beginning of March. The " George" Lettuce is a form of the " Gotte " but is larger in growth. The first " George " Lettuces are ready for planting in February on the beds or under cloches from which a crop of " Crêpe " Lettuces have been taken, the treatment as to watering, shading, protection from frost, and ventilation being the same as already described. The "*George*" Lettuces planted in February are generally fit for "pulling" by the end of March. At this period the "*George*" Lettuces may also be planted in the open air on a warm and sheltered border, the young plants having been previously raised and pricked out under cloches. These open-air Lettuces "heart up" during May.

THE "PALATINE" OR "RED" CABBAGE LETTUCE. —This Lettuce (fig. 42) with which may be associated

FIG. 42.—PALATINE CABBAGE LETTUCE.

other varieties known as the "All the Year Round" (*Merveille des Quatre Saisons*) and "Brown Champagne" (*brune de Champagne*)—is sown in the latter half of October under Cloches and on raised sloping beds, the treatment being precisely the same as for the "*Gotte*" and "*George*" Lettuces. Air is given freely on all favourable occasions when the young plants have become established, and the cloches are even taken off altogether on fine days so as to keep the plants strong and sturdy.

During March the young plants are taken from their winter quarters and transferred to warm sheltered borders; and towards the end of the same month or early in April plantations may be made in the open or on old beds. The soil beforehand should have been deeply dug and levelled, and if a good layer of old mould has been spread over it, so much the better. The plants are spaced out about a foot apart in straight lines, and should receive a good watering if the weather is fine, so as to settle the soil around the roots. This crop of Lettuces is generally fit to gather about the end of May.

Other sowings of the same varieties may be made at the end of February or early in March, and then every fortnight until August, in due course planting out about a foot apart, or intercropping with other vegetables. Such crops take from fifty to seventy days to mature, according to the season.

During the period of growth it will be necessary to run the hoe between the plants to stir up the soil, not only to keep the weeds down, but to encourage quicker growth. In the event of very dry weather, frequent waterings will be necessary, or a mulching from the old manure beds may be placed on the surface of the soil to retain the moisture.

Other Cabbage Lettuces that may be sown at the same time as the "Palatine" and treated in the same way, are "White - seeded All the Year Round" (*blonde d'été*) or "Royal," (fig. 43) an early and productive kind;

FIG. 43.—" ALL THE YEAR ROUND " CABBAGE LETTUCE.

"Brown Chavigny," a strong-growing kind; the "Large Brown Paresseuse" or "*Grise*" Lettuce of the Paris market-gardeners; and the "Brown Champagne "—all varieties of first-rate quality. With them may be associated the " Dutch Red " (*Rousse de Hollande*) and the " Presbytery " Lettuce.

English growers should bear in mind the difference in taste between French and English people. Generally speaking, brown or red-tinted Lettuces—no matter how excellent they may be—do not sell so readily in the English markets as they do in Paris.

" GRISE " OR LARGE BROWN PARESSEUSE LETTUCES. —Under these names the French market-gardeners grow thousands of Cabbage Lettuces, which are apparently the same as those known in England as " Giant Summer Lettuces " (fig. 44). The first crop is sown about the end of February or beginning of March on a hot-bed or in a frame. As there is no necessity for such care at this season of the year as is necessitated by

FIG. 44.—GRISE OR GIANT SUMMER
CABBAGE LETTUCE.

the autumn crops, the young plants may be transferred when ready direct from the seed-bed to their final quarters in the open frames. The labour of pricking out is thus saved. The plants are 15 to 18 in. apart, and during dry weather are kept well watered or mulched with old manure, so as to keep them crisp and tender. Sowings of " *Grise* " Lettuces may be made every fortnight until July, those during the summer being made in shady places in the open.

WINTER CABBAGE LETTUCES.—There are now about half a dozen kinds of Cabbage Lettuce grown in frames or under cloches during the winter months. Perhaps the best-known at present is that called the " Passion " —of which there are two varieties, the " Red " and the " White," so called from the colour of the foliage. The name of " Passion " Lettuce has been given simply because this va-riety is usually fit for gathering in Passion Week, *i.e.* second week be-fore Easter. When grown in the open air, "Passion" Let-tuces are not likely to be ready much

FIG. 45.—PASSION CABBAGE LETTUCE.

before May if the spring is cold and sunless (fig. 45).

Other kinds of winter Lettuces are " Large White Winter " (*blonde d'hiver*), a strong-growing variety that produces a very white and tender heart early in the season ; " Winter Brown " (*brune d'hiver*), a somewhat smaller variety, the outer leaves of which are washed with brown ; the ." Morine " or " Ham-mersmith Green Winter," a small sturdy Lettuce ; " Winter Red " (*rouge d'hiver*), a hardy variety with reddish foliage and a raised " heart " ; and " Winter Trémont " (fig. 46), which has a large, firm, very white heart, and outer leaves washed with rusty brown.

Culture.—" Passion " and other winter Lettuces may be sown from the middle of August to the middle of September. About a month after sowing, the young plants will be ready for pricking out in warm sheltered positions. In ordinary mild winters they require no special protection, nevertheless it is wise to have a supply of straw or litter handy in case of severe frosts, so that the plants can be covered up when necessary. According to the prevailing climatic conditions, the straw or litter is put on or taken off, bearing in mind that the more the plants

FIG. 46.—WINTER TRÉMONT CABBAGE LETTUCE.

are exposed to the light the better—otherwise they are apt to become pale in colour, and loose and flabby in habit.

II COS OR ROMAINE LETTUCES

The Cos Lettuces are quite distinct in form from the Cabbage varieties, and are always called " *Romaines* " or " *Chicons* " in France. There are many varieties, the following being generally considered the best by Parisian growers, viz. :

1. **Plate à cloches** (*syn.* Dwarf Frame Cos Lettuce), an early variety with leaves at first spreading.

2. **Blonde maraîchère** (*syn.* Paris White Cos), an

excellent Cos Lettuce, which hearts up quickly and is very extensively grown.

3. **Grise maraîchère** (*syn.* Paris Market Cos), a variety highly esteemed for cloche culture in the neighbourhood of Paris.

4. **Verte maraîchère** (*syn.* Green Paris Market), a variety not quite so large as the " *blonde maraîchère* " but somewhat earlier, and useful either for cloches or the open air. .

The first sowing of Cos or *Romaine* Lettuces under cloches may be made at the end of August, without the use of hot-beds. The soil should be deeply dug and well prepared, and afterwards covered with an inch or two of fine mould (old manure and gritty soil passed through a sieve). The surface is made flat and sufficiently firm either by patting with the back of the spade or a piece of board.

Imprints of a cloche are taken on the surface as many times as there are seed-beds to be sown. The seeds are then sown within the circumference of each, and lightly covered with fine soil, and gently watered.

Shading.—If the sun is too hot, the cloches covering the little seed-beds should be covered with mats to encourage quick germination. When this has taken place, however, the mats must be removed, and if the sun is still too strong a little whiting, chalk, or lime mixed up in water may be smeared over the cloches on the sunny side. The whitening of the cloches is to prevent the young plants from being scorched, and at the same time to allow sufficient light to percolate through the shading so that the leaves shall not turn yellow or become drawn. A little milk, or a piece of butter, added to the whiting, lime, or chalk will make the liquid adhere more firmly to the glass, and will not wash off with the first shower of rain.

The varieties of Cos Lettuce sown at this period are the " Dwarf Frame Cos " (known as *Plate à cloche*s) and the " Paris Market Cos " (*Grise maraîchère*). The last-named kind is chiefly useful for planting between the cloches that are covering plants of the first-named.

A well-known variety of Cos Lettuce, called " *verte maraîchère* " or " Green Paris Market Cos," is not now grown so largely by the market-gardeners of Paris as formerly, chiefly because it has failed to realise the best prices in market. It is, however, hardier than either *Plate à cloche*s or the *Grise maraîchère*, and in cold or bleak localities it may still be regarded as a profitable, and even desirable, crop.

Early in September, the seedlings will have developed two or three young leaves. They are then carefully pricked out under cloches, so as to be ready for planting in their final quarters in October. About twenty-four or thirty young plants are usually pricked out under each cloche, as shown in the diagrams (figs. 37–8). Early in October one Cos Lettuce is planted under each cloche, and not more than one, if the very best plants and prices are desired. Air is excluded for a few days after planting, and shading from strong sunshine may be necessary with mats, but once the plants have taken hold of the new ground, air may be given freely on all fine days—more than is usually given to Cabbage Lettuces at the same period.

At the beginning of November hot-beds should be prepared for Cos Lettuces that are to be " cloched." These beds are made of the hottest and best manure, to ensure a steady heat during the severe weather. In addition, it will be necessary, perhaps, to place dry manure between the cloches, and also to fill up the narrow pathways between the beds. Severe frosts at night must be kept out by double or treble coverings of mats if necessary.

When the beds are prepared, and covered with 4 or 5 in. of nice mould, one *Grise maraîchère* Cos Lettuce, and three "Black Gotte" Cabbage Lettuces are to be planted under each cloche, the Cos in the centre and the Cabbage Lettuces at the points of an equilateral triangle, as shown in fig. 47. These Lettuces are from seeds sown in September.

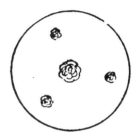

Fig. 47.

. It should be noted that the variety of Cos Lettuce known as "Dwarf Frame Cos" or "*Plate à cloches*" is considered unsuitable for planting with Cabbage Lettuces in the same way as "Paris Market Cos" (*Grise maraîchère*), because its leaves at first spread out so much towards the circumference of the cloche that the Cabbage Lettuces would not have a fair chance of developing. Towards maturity, however, the leaves rise up to the top of the cloche, and then bend inwards one over the other.

SPRING LETTUCES.—For spring crops seeds of Cos Lettuce are sown in the latter half of September, or early in October, in the open air, or on raised sloping beds, or under cloches. The plants are pricked out in due course, placing twenty-four or thirty under each cloche (see figs. 37-8). After shading and keeping close for a few days, air is then given on all favourable

occasions.   In the event of the plants becoming
" drawn," they should be taken up carefully, have the
old or dead leaves taken off, and be replanted immediately on a fresh bed, placing, however, only eighteen
or twenty plants under each cloche.   They are afterwards treated in a similar way to Cabbage Lettuces
sown at the same period.

At the end of December or early in January planting

NORTH.

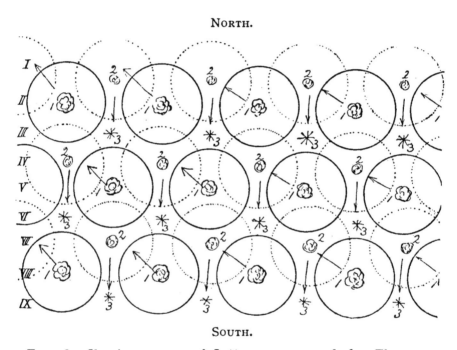

SOUTH.

FIG. 48.—Showing 9 rows of Lettuces on same bed.   The arrows
indicate how the Cloches are moved from Lettuces marked (1) to those,
marked (2) and afterwards to those marked (*3).

under cloches or lights takes place.   Under each cloche
one Cos and four Cabbage Lettuces may be planted,
as shown in the diagram (fig. 41), while Cos and Cabbage
Lettuces may be planted alternately in rows in the
frames.   Early in February these Lettuces are fit to
gather.   When the beds under the cloches and in the

frames have been cleared, the surface is prepared for a second crop.

About the end of February or early in March, if the weather is at all favourable, six rows of " Paris Market Cos " Lettuces (Grise maraîchère) may be planted between the cloches under each of which a Lettuce is already well established. It will be seen from the diagram that each row of cloches is flanked by two rows of Lettuces—one in front and one behind—and that the exposed Lettuces are planted in the spaces between the cloches. It thus happens that there are nine rows of Lettuces on each bed—six being open and three under cloches (see fig. 48).

As soon as the Lettuces marked (1) under cloches have been cut, the glasses thus rendered free are placed over the Lettuces in rows numbered (2) in the diagram—leaving rows of Lettuces numbered (3), of course, uncovered for the time being. When the No. 1 Lettuces are mature, which is generally about three weeks after covering, the cloches are then available for covering the plants in rows marked (2), which ripen about a fortnight afterwards. The cloches from rows marked (2) are then placed upon the rows marked *3.

The shifting of the cloches from one row on to another is done easily, and more expeditiously if the first cloche at the beginning is taken away to the other end of the bed. The vacant space thus left enables one to move the cloches forward (in what may be called a north-westerly direction, as shown in the diagram) so as to cover the required rows marked (2) as shown.

The last Lettuces from these beds become mature in April, or early in May, according to the mildness or otherwise of the season.

Borders.—When planting between the cloches in February or March in the way described above, it is also advisable to plant out rows of " Paris Market Cos " Lettuces (*Grise maraîchère*) on warm sheltered borders, allowing a foot of space between each plant.   These Lettuces are usually fit for market at the end of April or

during May.   After planting on the borders, some growers also sow seeds of Carrots, Radishes, and Leeks among the Cos Lettuces, and keep the whole bed well watered when necessary.

Another variety of Cos Lettuce called " Paris White " (*Blonde maraîchère*) is extensively cultivated in the F r e n c h market-gardens, and finds a ready sale.   It hearts up quickly, stands a good time, and is of fine quality (fig. 49).

FIG. 49.—COS LETTUCE " PARIS WHITE " (BLONDE MARAÎCHÈRE).

Seeds of this variety are usually sown in the latter half of October, the young plants being pricked out under cloches in the way already described.   When large enough they are planted under cloches.

SUMMER AND AUTUMN LETTUCES.—From the middle of March until the end of July or middle of August Lettuces are grown in the open air.   In March a sowing of " Giant Summer " Cabbage Lettuce (the *Grise* or *Grosse brune paresseuse*) (fig. 44) and " Paris White " Cos should be made, either under cloches or frames. When large enough about twenty young plants may be put under each light, or ten Cos Lettuces and ten Cabbage Lettuces may be planted alternately in the same space. When established, air must be given freely during genial weather, and attention must be paid to watering, so as to keep the plants tender and growing.

Every second or third week from March until August, seeds may be sown in the open air on nicely prepared soil. The seedlings are pricked out and transplanted in due course. The chief cultural details during the summer months consist of frequent hoeings between the plants and a plentiful supply of water. If the plants are allowed to suffer from drought they are almost sure to " bolt "—*i.e.* run to seed—during the summer months. They should therefore be copiously watered every day except when it rains heavily.

It is as well, however, to mention that watering is best done during the warm weather either in the morning or in the evening, as the wetting of plants exposed to the sun scorches the leaves and spoils their appearance.

For summer and autumn Lettuces the secret of success appears to be—sow the seeds thinly ; keep the young plants growing and tender by copious waterings ; and plant out as early as possible after the first true leaves form after the cotyledons or seed-leaves. Other varieties as well as those mentioned may of course be sown for summer and autumn crops.

Tying Cos Lettuces.—Although many varieties of Cos Lettuce hardly require tying at all, it generally pays to perform the operation, whether the plants are grown under cloches, frames, or in the open. It

makes them swell earlier, and gives a greater purity
and crispness to the hearts. The tying is done when
the plants have made three-fourths of their growth,
and the material used may be raffia or rye grass. If
steeped in water for about twenty minutes the tying
material becomes more pliable and is more easily
handled, even by experts.

Diseases and Pests.—Lettuces under intensive cultivation are subject to attacks from numerous pests and
diseases. Amongst the most common insect pests are
aphides, or green fly, which attack the plants at the
" collar "—the point where the leaves and roots join.
The Cock-chafer Grub (*Melolontha vulgaris*) preys upon
the roots. The soil should be searched as soon as the
leaves of a plant are seen to droop, and very often
the grub will be found at the base. Wireworms (*Elater
lineatus*) and other grubs also play havoc with the
plants in the open air, and can only be kept in check
by the use of traps made of pieces of potato or carrot,
which should be examined frequently.

Mildew (*Peronospora gangliformis*)—the " meunier "
or miller of the French gardener—is one of the worst
pests amongst early Lettuces, and where it is anticipated, the young plants, and also the surrounding soil,
should be sprinkled with flowers of sulphur. A weak
solution of sulphate of copper has also been found
useful as a preventive by watering the soil after sowing
the seeds, or before planting out the seedlings. The
same remedy applies to the rust fungus that also attacks
Lettuces. About 1 lb. sulphate of copper to 100 pints
of water makes a good solution. Where young
Lettuces are attacked with mildew, the wisest course
to adopt is to lift the plants carefully and burn them,

afterwards mending the rows with healthy plants from the seed-bed. If a little more sand or grit were mixed with the mould on the surface, it is possible that mildew would not be so prevalent amongst early Lettuces as it is, when the old mould only is used.

*Slug*s are also very fond of young Lettuces, but may be checked by sprinkling powdered lime and soot over the plants and soil on several successive evenings or early mornings.

MELONS

The cultivation of early Melons (*Cucumis Melo*) forms one of the greatest industries in Parisian market-gardens. Every one in Paris, apparently, eats Melons, and when the fruits are cheap in August—about 2*d*. or 3*d*. per lb.—one may see great barrow-loads of them being hawked in the street, where they sell readily. Early in the season, however, similar fruits realise as much as 20*s*. to 25*s*. in Paris, while even the " second choice " fetch 6*s*. or 8*s*. each.

The varieties grown are quite distinct from the netted varieties one is accustomed to see in English hothouses. The French people prefer what are known as " Cantaloup " Melons, and the varieties which find most favour with the market-gardeners of Paris are those known as " Cantaloup Early Frame " or *Prescott hatif à châssis* (fig. 50) and *Prescott fond blanc*. The latter is a strong-growing variety, with large roundish compressed fruits, often nearly a foot in diameter, with irregular ribs and

FIG. 50.—PRESCOTT EARLY FRAME MELON.

furrows, and a mottled grey-green and yellowish appearance when ripe. The flesh is reddish, and the flavour is excellent. A Silver variety called " *argenté* " (fig. 51) is also much grown. Another form, *Prescott fond gris*, is often seen in the French markets.

The "Cantaloup" Melon was introduced from Armenia to Italy about the fifteenth century, and was brought into France in 1495 by Charles VIII.

Culture.—To obtain the first-early crops of Melons,

FIG. 51.—CANTALOUP SILVERY PRESCOTT.

seeds are sown in January. The plants from these, however, require frames heated with hot-water pipes as well as manure, as the chief trouble during the winter months is to secure as much light as possible for the plants.

The cultivation of early " Cantaloup " Melons may well be recommended to those market nurserymen in the British Islands who have already suitable glass-houses well equipped with hot-water apparatus. If seeds are sown about the middle of November, it is possible to secure nice fruits (which would probably command high prices) about the end of March. The seeds for this purpose should be well ripened and saved from fruits of the preceding year, to secure the best results.

The main crop in frames is generally sown in February and March. A hot-bed 2½ to 3 ft. thick is made of quite fresh and old manure in equal proportions. It is trodden down and made firm and level, and if necessary well watered. Then, before placing the frame upon it, thè bed is covered with 6 to 8 in. of fine and rich gritty mould that has been passed through a sieve. The frame is placed in position, and is banked up or " lined " all round with a good layer of manure to keep the cold out and the heat constant within.

When the heat of the bed has sunk to 75° or 80° F., the seeds are sown about 1 in. apart in shallow drills. They are lightly covered with soil, and gently watered. For two or three days—until the seeds begin to sprout— the frame is kept close and covered with mats. After germination, the mats are taken off during the day-time, but placed on again at night, and a little air is given for an hour or two each day when the weather is genial.

Should the temperature within the frame fall below 68° or 70° F., the old manure outside the frame must be removed, and fresh hot manure should take its place.

At the end of fourteen or eighteen days, when the seed-leaves are well developed, another hot-bed to accommodate a three-light frame should be made up in the same way as the first. The young Melons are then either pricked out of the seed-bed into the new soil about 4 or 5 in. apart, making a hole with the finger instead of a dibber, or, better still, each one is placed in a 3-in. pot, using a compost of rich gritty loam and a little leaf soil. When the young plants are being put into pots, they should be handled carefully so as not to injure the roots too much, and the soil also should not be pressed too firmly around them. Whether the plants are pricked out or potted up, care should be taken in either case to bury the young stems in the soil up to the seed-leaves.

After potting, the young plants should be " plunged " in the compost up to the rim of the pots, before which they should have been watered with a fine-rosed water-pot to settle the soil.

Another method of treating the seedling Melons is as follows: A 3-in. pot is taken and a wisp of straw or litter is twisted round it firmly so as to acquire the shape. Pot and straw are then placed where the young Melons are to grow—as many pots and wisps of straw being used as are necessary, and placed firmly side by side. When finished a gentle twist and pull of the pot will free it from the straw, in which a hole or pocket corresponding to the form of the pot is left. Each hole is then filled with rich loamy compost, in which the young Melon is planted. The advantage of this method appears to be that when the roots have absorbed the nourishment from the soil surrounding them, they are then at liberty to pierce their way through the litter in search of more, whereas in pots they would be unable to travel in this way.

Whichever method is employed, it is essential to keep the lights covered with mats for three or four days until the young plants recover from the shifting. Afterwards, the mats are taken off during the day, and a little air is given in genial weather by tilting the lights on one side or another, or at the top or bottom according to the direction of the wind—always taking care to open only on the leeward side.

Pinching.—When the plants have developed three or four leaves (beyond the seed-leaves) the stem is pinched off about an inch or a little more, beyond the second leaf ; and the seed-leaves themselves are also suppressed, so that when decaying they shall not injure the main stem. Pinching should always be done before the young Melons are planted out finally, as it would be unwise to injure the tops and bottoms of the plants at the same time. After the pinching process, a little air should be given, just for two or three hours in the middle of the day during mild or sunny weather. If necessary, slight sprinklings with tepid water may also be given, but one must guard against too much moisture and too much air at this particular period.

Planting.—When the two side branches that usually result from the first pinching have two or three leaves each, the plants are then ready for placing in their fruiting quarters.

When several rows of frames are being used for Melon culture, the beds are made in the following way : In the first row of frames, the soil is taken out about 2ft. wide and 1 ft. deep, and placed outside the beds or moved to the end where the last trench is to be made. The trench is then filled with two-thirds fresh manure and one-third old manure, all well mixed and trodden down. The first bed being thus made, the soil from the trench in the second bed is spread over it evenly.   In the same way after the trench in the second bed has been filled with manure, the soil from the third bed is spread over it ; and so on till all the beds are made.

When the heat has sunk to about 75° or 80° Fahr., two or three Melon plants are then placed under each light in the centre of the frame.   A hole is scooped out of the compost with the hands and a young Melon plant is carefully turned out of its pot or lifted from its position with a nice ball of soil.   Each plant is carefully placed in the hole thus made, arranging one shoot to point to the top of the frame and the other towards the bottom.   Injury to the roots must be avoided, and the mould should be packed round them carefully by hand.

A little tepid water is then given to each plant, the frames are closed up and shaded with mats for three or four days until the plants have recovered.   When they show signs of new growth, the mats may be taken off during the day unless the sun gets too hot. They are, however, put on again at night-time for protection.

Ventilation and Watering.—About a week after planting a little air may be given, very little at first, but gradually increasing the amount as the weather becomes warmer and the plants stronger.   Attention must be paid to watering, the supply being regulated largely by the vigour of growth and the weather. When the plants are growing freely and the weather is warm, more water will be required than when reverse conditions prevail.   About the end of May, or during June, if the weather is fine the lights may be taken off the plants altogether during the daytime. They should, however, be handy to cover up immediately in case of a sudden storm or a dangerous fall in the temperature.

Stopping or Pinching.—When the side shoots (that were stopped some time before planting) are a foot or more in length, it will be necessary to pinch out the tops of each an inch or so beyond the third, fourth, or even fifth leaf, according to the vigour of the shoots. This stopping causes side shoots to develop from each branch, but these shoots or " laterals " must be also checked in their turn.

At this stage it is a good plan to spread straw or litter over the bed before new branches develop.

In due course side shoots will appear on the branches that were last " stopped " by pinching. When about a foot long this third set of shoots should also be pinched back a little above the third leaf. At this stage any flowers on the shoots should be suppressed, as they are generally male (or staminate) blossoms and are quite useless for the formation of Melons. If by chance the shoots are bearing any female (or pistillate) flowers—easily recognised by the roundish swelling behind the corolla—these are also best destroyed, as the plants are still too young and lack the necessary force to develop fruits worth having from these first blossoms.

After this stopping and pinching, as growth continues, a watch is kept for the appearance of female flowers. When the young fruits are forming behind these, a selection of those best situated should be made. Those on the main stem or too near the centre of the plant should be removed. Later on, when the fruits are about as large as a hen's or even a pigeon's egg, two of the very best are selected and all the others are taken off the plant. When the fruits have grown somewhat larger—say about the size of a cricket ball or a man's fist—the shoots bearing them should be shortened back an inch or so beyond the leaf in front of the fruit, so that the sap may be drawn as far as this without being wasted.

The best fruit on each plant is then decided upon—whether it be on the shoot pointing to the top of the frame or on the shoot pointing to the bottom—and the other is suppressed. One fruit only is thus allowed to ripen on each plant, as it is considered better to have one large fine fruit than two smaller ones.

As each pinching and stopping of the shoots causes a certain amount of injury, it is well to give the plants a slight sprinkling and to keep them shaded from bright sunshine for a day or two.

As the fruits increase in size and weight it is a good plan to place a piece of glass, slate, or board beneath each one so that the under-side shall not become dis-coloured. Uniformity of colour may also be secured by slightly turning the fruits from time to time, or by standing them upright on their stalks.

Occasionally a fruit is inclined to become irregular or deformed. This may be avoided or overcome by making a vertical and transverse slit in the skin, (thus : +) in the place where there is a hollow. The effect of these slits is to draw the sap to the injured portion, thus causing it to fill up the hollow that at first seemed imminent.

During the development of the fruits, attention is given to watering and ventilation. While the soil must be kept moist and the plants kept growing steadily, care must be taken not to give too much water; and the water itself should be tepid or of the same temperature at least as the atmosphere in the frame. Watering is always best done in the morning —say before ten o'clock—before the sun becomes too powerful to scorch the wetted foliage; otherwise it should be done late in the afternoon.

Under certain conditions, as, for instance, when the plants are growing more vigorously than usual, and are inclined to develop too many shoots and leaves, water should be withheld almost entirely, or given only very sparingly. This causes a check to the growth of stems and leaves, and results in better development of the fruits.

Late Crops.—For a later crop of Melons, seeds should be sown in April. It will not be necessary, however, at that period of the year to go to the trouble of making up such deep hot-beds as was necessary for the earlier crops, as the weather is far more genial, and the prevailing temperature is naturally higher. Having marked out the place to be occupied by the frames, a trench in the centre about 18 in. wide and 1 ft. deep is taken out with the spade. The trench is then filled with good fresh manure that has been previously well turned over. When trodden down, it is covered with a layer of nice mould about 6 in. deep taken from the adjoining frames; and so on with each bed in succession.

Rotation.—It should be borne in mind that it is not good practice to grow Melons two years running on the same ground. The principles of rotation should be applied to intensive cultivation, as the benefits arising therefrom are just as great as in the open ground.

Gathering the Fruit.—It is important to know exactly when a Melon fruit is fit to cut from the plant. If left too long, or cut before the proper time, a loss may result to the grower. The best time to cut the fruit is when the skin commences to change colour. Fruits cut at this time should be placed in a cool, dark, airy place where they will ripen gradually without losing in quality or flavour. When the fruits assume a distinctly yellow tinge they should be eaten without delay.

MELONS UNDER CLOCHES.—The kinds best suited for growing under cloches are known as " *Chypre* " or " *Kroumi*r," although the " Prescott " varieties may be also grown.

Seeds are sown early in April on hot-beds prepared as for the " Prescott " varieties (see p. 169), and in ten or fifteen days the young plants are fit to be pricked out on beds about 1 ft. in thickness. They may be covered either with frames or cloches. By the first or second week in May the young plants will be large enough to transfer to their fruiting quarters. A trench about 2 ft. wide and 1 ft. deep is prepared, and filled with good manure. Over this 6 or 8 in. of good rich loam and leaf soil is placed, and the Melons are carefully planted about 2 ft. apart. Each one is covered with a cloche, and air and light are excluded for several days until the plants recover. Shading is done either with mats or by white-washing the cloches on the sunny side.

About a week or a fortnight after planting—according to the weather and the state of the plant—a little air may be given, gradually raising the cloche more and more on the tilt as the plants increase in size and vigour.

About the end of May the cloche is no longer large enough to hold the entire plant. The branches must, therefore, be allowed to run outside as soon as weather permits.

Some straw or litter may be spread over the beds before this to keep them moist, and the cloches may be raised off the soil by placing three small pots or tilts beneath them. In this way the main stem will be protected against cold or against heavy waterings or drenching rains.

The tips of the shoots are pinched in the same way as recommended for the "Prescott" varieties (see p. 173), but eight or nine leaves may be left on the two branches that develop after the first stem has been stopped. The shoots arising from these two branches should be shortened to four leaves ; and the branches arising from these, again, may be shortened to three leaves.

As soon as fruits appear a selection should be made of the best. Those that are allowed to ripen should be protected by cloches, or each fruit at least should be covered with a large leaf to protect it from the sun. About the middle of July the cloches may be removed altogether if the weather is fine, and early in August the "*Chypre*" or "*Kroumir*" Melons should be ripe.

Diseases.--Melons are afflicted occasionally with several diseases. The worst apparently in French gardens is the "nuile"---a disease which causes the leaves, young stems, and fruits to rot. It is brought about by a fungus known as *Scolecotrichum mcloph-*

thorum, and is due to cold, wet, and erratic seasons, and is checked naturally by keeping the plants warm and dry during such periods, and dusting with flowers of sulphur. *Canker* sometimes attacks the plants and is best cured by cutting away the injured portions, and rubbing powdered lime or ashes on the wounds. Black Aphis, Red Spider, and Thrips are best checked by frequently syringing the under-surface of the leaves with a quassia-chip and soft-soap solution, or any of the advertised insecticides.

MUSHROOMS

A treatise on French market-gardening would be scarcely complete without some reference to the French method of cultivating Mushrooms. The system of culture adopted by growers in the outskirts of Paris differs in so many ways from that practised in England, that it may be worth while recording it somewhat fully. Last summer (1908) I had the pleasure of meeting a Parisian mushroom grower, and he very kindly showed me not only his own " cultures," but also introduced me to some friends of his in the neighbourhood of Montrouge.

It has been estimated by M. Curé—a writer on French market-gardening—that 10,000,000 francs (or £400,000) are earned by the cultivation of Mushrooms and the sale of old beds every year in the neighbourhood of Paris alone. This is sufficient to indicate what an important industry mushroom-growing is, and also accounts for the establishment of the " Syndicat des Champignonnistes," a society formed to protect the interests of mushroom-growers in France. The British mushroom-grower—or " Champignonniste," as he ought to call himself perhaps—prefers to work out his salvation on independent, instead of on co-operative lines, and has, therefore, something yet to learn from his French competitor.

In the neighbourhood of Paris Mushrooms are mostly grown in underground quarries from which stone has

FIG. 52.—MUSHROOM-BEDS IN CAVE: ROOF
SUPPORTED BY BLOCKS OF STONE.

been excavated in years gone by. These quarries, or carrières, are from 60 to 80 ft. below the surface, a fact that ensures a fairly equable temperature—from 60° to 70° Fahr.—all the year round. Some of these quarries are entered by a sloping roadway, but admission to many is only obtained by descending a more or less shaky pole, with rungs thrust through it to make a ladder. It is like descending an old and deep well, and it is with some trepidation and curiosity that the stranger makes his first descent in this way.

Arrived at the bottom one finds himself in a large opening, from which what look like dark tunnels radiate in every direction. Small lamps, fixed to a stick about 18 in. long, are used to enable the workmen to see what they are doing. Colza oil is now burned in these little lamps in preference to paraffin, as it was found that the fumes from the latter caused headaches and other troubles that prevented the workmen from attending to their duties for more than two or three hours at a time.

The tunnels or galleries are just as they were left by the quarrymen, except where the mushroom-growers have collected irregular masses of stone and piled them up as supports to the roof, or to fill some great gap in the side walls. The general appearance is well shown in the accompanying illustrations (figs. 52, 53), from *The Parks and Gardens of Paris*.

Fresh air—being essential, not only for human life but also for the sake of the Mushrooms—is secured by lighting fires beneath some of the openings that communicate with the outer air. This causes an upward current at one place and a downward current at another, and in this way the air is constantly kept in a fresh state—as in a coal mine.

It is no easy matter traversing these mushroom galleries, as many of them are only a few feet wide, and often only 4 or 5 ft. high. The inky blackness is only just dispelled by the glow from the lamp, while one has to plant his feet carefully on the ground to avoid slipping on the wet or greasy and irregular floors.

The manure used for these mushroom beds is the best that can be got from the Parisian stables. It is brought to the mouth of the caves overhead, and thrown down to the bottom. Here it is mixed and turned, and brought into the proper state for making up the beds. These run along the floors and at the base of the walls of the tunnels, and vary in length according to the space available. Sometimes several beds run side by side, •as shown in fig. 53, with only a narrow alley between them wide enough to allow

FIG. 53.—VIEW IN OLD UNDERGROUND STONE QUARRIES NOW DEVOTED TO GROWING MUSHROOMS.

a man to walk by putting one foot in front of the other. Each bed is generally about 18 in. wide at the base, and about 18 in. high, tapering upwards so that the top is only about 4 in. wide.

In such restricted places, it is obvious that carrying or wheeling the manure from one place to another is by no means easy work, and there is always plenty to do. As soon as beds cease to produce a crop the old manure is taken away and hauled up to the surface ; and fresh manure is brought in for new beds.

12 *

The beds themselves are made up by placing the prepared manure in heaps and layers, and then pressing it firmly with the feet and knees until the required degree of solidity is secured. All loose pieces of manure or litter are then " combed " away from the surface with the hands, to give a finished and tidy appearance.

When the temperature has sunk to 80° Fahr. the beds are ready for " spawning." This work is generally done by a more experienced workman. He breaks the loose cake of spawn into pieces about 3 or 4 in. square, and pushes each piece well into the manure-bed about 6 in. from the other.

The beds thus " spawned " are then ready to be " cased over " with a layer of soil. The Parisian growers prefer for this purpose a mixture of rich loamy soil and mortar rubble, or old plaster of Paris. This is passed through a half-inch sieve, and is well mixed up in advance. A layer of this compost, from 1½ to 2½ in. thick, is then spread over the beds with a little flat wooden shovel, the back of which is used to make the surface even and regular.

Two or three weeks after these various operations have been performed satisfactorily, the young Mushrooms begin to appear on the surface of the soil. When large enough—2 in. or a little more across the tops—they are picked and sent to market.

In these Parisian caves, owing, no doubt, to the equable temperature and the proper degree of humidity in the atmosphere, the beds will produce mushrooms for eight or nine weeks, and often longer under very favourable circumstances. The mushrooms are picked every day, and not once or twice a week, as in the case of larger beds made in the open air ; and as the prices vary from 6d. to 2s. per lb., according to circumstances and seasons, one may form some idea as to whether the industry is remunerative or not. At the same time the enormous expenses entailed in the production must not be overlooked.

It sometimes happens that the beds become too dry. They are then moistened with tepid water ; and it is necessary to apply it by means of a fine-rosed water-can, so that the soil shall not be broken down from the manure it is encasing.

Diseases.—The mushroom-growers of Paris have to contend with a fungoid disease called the " molle " that attacks the Mushrooms—sometimes so badly that the caves have to be abandoned for some time, and thoroughly cleaned out. One of the chief causes of trouble, apparently, is the lack of fresh air. It is, therefore, of the greatest importance that fires should be kept going constantly so that the air in remote ends of the tunnels may be kept as pure as possible.

Tiny black flies, like Pear-midges or mites, often find their way into the mushroom caves, and play havoc with the crop occasionally. The best way to get rid of them is to burn sulphur or brimstone in the caves before starting a new crop.

Preparation of Mushroom Spawn.—The spawn used by the Parisian grower is quite different in appearance from that used in England. Here the spawn is made up in solid bricks or cakes, 8 or 9 in. long, 4 or 5 in. wide, and about $1\frac{1}{2}$ in. in thickness—a fair quantity of cow-manure being used in its preparation. In Paris, on the other hand, cow-manure is never used for making mushroom spawn. Only the best horse-manure is used, and bricks or cakes of spawn are much looser and lighter than the English ones.

Almost every grower in Paris prepares his own spawn in the following way : In the month of July some good manure is turned over a few times until it becomes short and crisp, and well heated, just in the same condition as for making up mushroom beds. A trench about 2 ft. wide and 2 ft. deep is then dug out in a shady place—generally in some position facing north. Some small pieces of spawn are then placed about a foot apart in two rows along the bottom of the trench thus made, from one end to the other. After this the trench is filled up with the prepared manure, and this is trodden down firmly with the feet. The soil taken out of the trench is now spread over the manure in the trench. A piece of board, however, is placed near the centre of the trench, before the soil is placed on top, and this may be lifted up when it is desired to see what progress the spawn is making in the manure beneath. Three or four weeks, as a rule, are allowed for the spawn to spread throughout the manure in the trench. The soil is then removed, and the compressed manure, now saturated with the mycelium or spawn of the mushrooms, is cut into flat cakes. These are spread out in cool, dry, airy sheds or barns, on shelves made of battens, where they remain until required for use.

This seems such a simple and clean method of preparing mushroom spawn that it is a wonder it is not adopted in England. It is, of course, possible that as most of our Mushrooms are grown in beds in the open air, spawn in horse-manure would not last nearly so long in our climate as that prepared with the addition of cow-manure.

Another method of preparing mushroom-spawn has been adopted by the Pasteur Institute in Paris. Briefly, it consists in developing the spawn or mycelium direct from the spores of the mushroom. The best specimens are selected and placed on sheets of paper. As the spores ripen on the "gills," or lamellæ, of the mushroom, they fall on the surface of the paper, and if undisturbed, mark the outline of the mushroom cap. Some manure, nicely prepared as described above, and a few mushroom spores, are then placed in a test tube, the mouth of which is hermetically sealed. The tube is placed in a warm stove, the spores germinate readily, and in about a fortnight the mycelium threads (or spawn) have spread throughout the manure in the test tube. "Spawn" obtained in this way has been used for the production of Mushrooms, but it is said that the results, so far, have not been quite so satisfactory as were anticipated.

ONIONS

Although there are many varieties of Onion (*Allium Cepa*) in cultivation, there is now only one specially adapted for intensive cultivation as practised by the Parisians market-gardeners, that is, the variety known as "*Blanc hâtif de Paris*," or "Early White Paris." Formerly another variety, the "*Jaune des Vertus*," was extensively cultivated, but has been discarded as it is not sufficiently remunerative.

Seeds are sown in beds about the middle of August. If sown earlier, or at least before August 15, in

Paris, the plants are liable to run to seed instead of developing bulbs. The soil should be deeply dug and well prepared, and the seeds should be sown fairly thickly, after the soil has been pressed down with the feet, especially if inclined to be " light " or gritty. A good watering should be given after the seeds have been worked into the soil with the rake, and a light covering of mould has been spread over the surface of the seed-bed. This will hasten germination. As dry weather often prevails at this period, the seed-bed should be watered frequently if necessary, as the sprouting seeds would be fatally injured by a spell of drought.

In September or early in October the young plants will be ready for pricking out of the seed-bed into beds of fine rich and gritty soil. The plants are lifted by passing a spade horizontally beneath the roots, so that these may not be injured. The best seedlings are then selected one by one, and the inferior ones are thrown away. A small bunch is made so that the baby bulbs are all level. Then the roots are cut back within half an inch or so of the bulbs, and the leaves also are cut back leaving only 2 or 3 in. —the whole plant after shortening being only about 4 in. altogether from one extremity to the other. Onions treated in this way are carefully placed in a basket with the bulbs lying the same way. When as many plants as are required for one day's planting have been thus prepared, the basket containing them is immersed in water, so that the injured plants may be freshened up somewhat. The Parisian gardeners carry out this practice with all the plants during hot weather, even if it happens to rain. If by chance it is not possible to plant all the Onions the same day as they have been prepared, they are covered with a board on which a fairly heavy weight is placed. This is to keep the plants straight ; otherwise they would be likely to curl or twist, and this would make it more difficult to plant them, and also hinder them becoming established quickly afterwards.

These *blanc hâtif* or " Early White Onions " are at first planted very• thickly by market-gardeners, who allow little more than 1 or 1½ in. between them. Great care is taken not to plant too deeply, about ¾ in. deep being considered quite deep enough for all kinds of Onions. If planted much deeper, the plants do not develop so freely or so well. Some growers plant the young Onions in rows, allowing 3 or 4 in. from plant to plant. In either case they are not allowed to reach their full size, but are sold as soon as the bulbs are an appreciable size. In this way the Onions are cleared as quickly as possible and the soil becomes available for another crop.

During October seedling Onions may be pricked out in the way described, but if the work is not finished by the first week in November, it is advisable to leave the plants in the seed-beds until the following February, as the winter frosts would be almost sure to kill transplanted seedlings.

In the event of severe weather setting in before the plants have taken a good hold, it is advisable to protect them at night with a sprinkling of straw or litter, taking this off as early as possible in the morning. About the end of April, or early in May, these autumn sown Onions are fit for market, coming into use at the same time as the " Ox-Heart " Cabbages (see p. 92).

If a further supply of early Onions is required, or if the rows have to be " made up " where plants of the previous sowing have failed, seeds are sown again—to provide for these contingencies—in January and February. At this season the seeds are sown on hot-beds under lights, or under cloches, and sometimes between other crops. The plants will be ready some-what later than those sown in August, but they will make a good succession crop.

Many growers also sow seeds of the " Early White " (*blanc hâtif*) Onion at intervals from February to June in the open air. The beds are dug, manured, and prepared in the usual way, and after the seeds have been sown a layer of nice rich mould is spread over the surface of each bed. When the Onions appear they are " thinned out " in due course, if too thick. Afterwards they are watered well from time to time when necessary, according to the state of the weather. As soon as the young bulbs begin to swell, they are almost ready for pulling, as it does not pay to leave them to mature on ground for which high rents have to be paid. An excellent little Onion for spring sowing is the *blanc très hâtif de la Reine* (Early White Queen). When sown in March it is ready in May, but as it is little more than an inch when fully developed, it is grown more in private than in market gardens.

RADISHES

There are now many varieties of small Radishes (*Raphanus sativus*) suitable for cultivation either in the open air or on hot-beds with other crops. They vary in colour from the purest white to the deepest crimson, passing through light and dark rose, and

almost scarlet. Growers for market, however, generally confine themselves to a few well-established
varieties. For early crops the Turnip or Round red
forms—known to us as " Forcing Scarlet " Radishes—
are favoured (fig. 54). These are followed with the
" French Breakfast " and white-tipped kinds (fig. 55),
and after these it really matters little which variety is
grown.

The first sowing of Radishes is made about the
middle of September. Raised sloping beds are pre-

FIG. 54.—FORCING SCARLET WHITE-TIPPED RADISH.

pared as described at p. 12, and the seeds are then
sown broadcast and covered with about an inch of
fine gritty soil. At night-time if frosts are likely to
occur, mats or litter are placed over the beds for
protection, and taken off each morning as early as
possible. Radishes from this sowing are generally
fit to pull about the end of November or early in
December.

In December Radishes (round red varieties) are
sown under lights on nicely prepared soil, and often
among other crops such as Carrots, Cauliflowers,
Lettuces, and Leeks—all of which require air to be
given in the same way as the Radishes.

When sown with other crops, it is better to sow Radishes in little patches between them rather than broadcast. Each little patch will yield a dozen or two of Radishes, which, as they develop rapidly, do not harm either Carrots, Lettuces, or Cauliflowers.

Early in February, or at the end of January, Radishes are sown again on open beds—*i.e.* beds not covered with lights. These beds are made up of

FIG. 55.—OLIVE-SCARLET WHITE-TIPPED RADISH.

manure 12 to 15 in. deep, on the surface of which about 4 in. of fine mould is spread. The seeds are covered with about an inch of soil, and mats or litter are afterwards spread over them to hasten germination. After this, as much light as possible must be given, but if frost is anticipated at night, the beds must be protected with mats or litter. The Rose variety with white tips, " French Breakfast," and the " Early Red Scarlet " are the best varieties for sowing on beds.

At this period thick sowings of Radishes may also be made on warm sheltered borders, and protected from frosts with mats or litter when necessary. Sowings in the open air may be made fortnightly until about the middle of September or October—according to the season. It is not essential to sow them in beds by themselves. The spaces between the rows of Lettuces or Cauliflowers may be utilised when these plants are still small and not too close together.

To secure nice Radishes, they should be sown in rich moist soil, and during the hot summer days a good watering in the morning and in the evening will be highly beneficial. As Radishes mature in from twenty-five to thirty days after sowing, one may judge when they are to be sown on any vacant spaces.

In sowing Radishes there is one important point to bear in mind if nice roots are desired, and that is that the seeds should be sown somewhat deeper than most other small seeds. In other words, they should be covered more thickly with fine mould—say about an inch thick—to encourage them to develop regularly and symmetrically. Being embedded in the soil in this way the skin retains its colour, and the Radishes do not become hard, hot and woody, as they are likely to do when the seeds are only slightly covered with soil.

It is, perhaps, scarcely necessary to mention that all early sowings of Radishes in the open air require protection from the depredation of birds, by means of fish-netting, black cotton or other devices.

BLACK RADISHES.—In the Paris markets a black-skinned Radish is frequently seen. The roots are something like the pointed "Croissy" Turnip in shape, and look as if they had been rolled in dry soot. They are about 6 in. long, tapering to a fine tip. The two varieties of Black Radish best known are "Round Winter" and the "Long Winter."

SALSAFY AND SCORZONERA

Salsafy (*Tragopogon porrifolium*) and Scorzonera (*Scorzonera hispanica*)—two members of the Chicory and Dandelion family—now find their way into the English markets in small quantities, and are valued chiefly for their long thickish roots. These are white in Salsafy and blackish in Scorzonera. The former is a biennial, and in growth has long narrow grey-green leaves with a whitish midrib, and produces violet flowers. Scorzonera, on the other hand, is a perennial, has broad lance-shaped oblong leaves, and bright yellow flowers.

Both plants are cultivated in almost precisely the same way, and if the soil has been deeply dug and well manured in advance, nice shapely roots are produced. In March or April the seeds are sown in shallow drills about a foot apart. When the seedlings are about 2 in. high, they should be thinned out about 4 in. apart. During the season growth is encouraged by frequent hoeings and copious supplies of water, especially in hot, dry weather. This will prevent the Salsafy plants running to seed, and thus failing to produce roots.

About October the roots are lifted, and if stored in sand or dry soil will remain fit for use during the winter months. As Scorzonera is a hardier plant than Salsafy, its roots may be left in the soil, giving protection if necessary from severe frosts with litter, etc.

For market purposes the roots of both Salsafy and Scorzonera are tied up into neat bundles. They are used in a boiled state, and those of Salsafy are popularly known as " Vegetable Oyster."

SORREL

It is astonishing the amount of Sorrel (*Rumex Acetosa*) that is grown and consumed in Paris. In the markets large bundles of bright green leaves are always seen, and women are often engaged in picking them off and grading them according to size and freshness. For over five centuries Sorrel has been a favourite dish with the French, and yet it is scarcely known in British gardens.

There are several varieties, but those with large juicy leaves are the best. Those known as " *large de Belleville* " (or " Broad-leaved Belleville "), " *Lyon*s," and " *blonde de Sarcelle*s " are grown, as well as others.

A variety, however, called " Maiden " or Dutch Sorrel (*Oseille vierge*) has become noteworthy. It is supposed to be a form of *Rumex montanu*s instead of *R. Aceto*sa, and has large round leaves. As it rarely flowers or seeds, the popular name " Maiden " (*vierge*) has been given to it. It grows in strong tufts and continues to produce luscious leaves for many years. It is generally propagated by dividing the tufts, while the other kinds of Sorrel are raised from seeds when necessary.

Early Sorrel can only be secured by forcing established clumps in hot-beds. These are prepared early in November, with a temperature of 55° to 60° Fahr. After placing the frames in position a couple of inches of mould is spread over the surface. The Sorrel plants are then lifted from the open ground with a fork, and after the crowns have been cleaned from old leaves

13

and stems, they are placed side by side in the frames, putting the larger or taller clumps near the top, and the smaller or shorter at the bottom. Some fine rich gritty mould is then worked in between and slightly over the crowns, and is settled down with a gentle watering. After growth commences all that is necessary is to give occasional moistenings with tepid water, and ventilation according to the state of the weather.

When the leaves are large enough they should be picked by hand every third or fourth day—the largest always being picked first. About eight days after placing in the hot-bed, the plants commence to yield, and will continue to produce tender leaves for a month or six weeks, according to their vigour. When the plants cease to develop leaves they may be thrown away; others are then lifted and placed in their stead.

Another method of obtaining early Sorrel is to force the plants where they are growing instead of lifting them and placing in hot-beds. The Sorrel is planted in beds wide enough to take the lights and frames generally in use. The plantation should have been made originally in deeply dug or trenched and heavily manured soil. As a rule each Sorrel bed has five rows of plants—the two outer ones being about 6 in. from the margins and the others equidistant from each other.

In the first half of November the plants are cleared of old leaves and stems, and the frames are placed over them. About half an inch of rich gritty soil is then spread uniformly over the crowns, and well watered in before the lights are put on.

The pathways between the beds are afterwards dug out 8 to 10 in. deep, the soil being placed at the end of the rows until it is again required. The trenches thus made in the pathways are filled with three parts of fresh manure to one part of old manure or leaves. The heat generated from the manure in the pathways causes the Sorrel plants to grow, and forcing has commenced. Watering with tepid water occasionally, and giving more or less air according to the state of the weather, constitute the principal points to which attention must be given.

About fifteen or eighteen days after the manure has been placed between the frames, leaves will be ready to pick and will continue to appear for about two months. Sorrel beds forced in this way will give a fair yield the second year, but afterwards the plants do not possess sufficient vitality to give a reasonable crop.

When the crop is finished, the manure is removed from the trenches, and these are refilled with the soil taken from them at first, after which the frames and lights are used for other purposes, and the Sorrel bed is again open to the air.

SEAKALE

Seakale (*Crambe maritima*)—the "*Chou marin*" of the French growers—although now so extensively cultivated by market-gardeners in England for the blanched leaf-stalks, is curiously enough not yet a great article of commerce in France, owing probably to the difficulty in securing sufficiently large tracts of land, that are so necessary to raise a quantity of plants for forcing purposes. The English method of cultivation may be briefly described as follows :

An open sunny situation is essential, and the soil for Seakale should be trenched 2 to 3 ft. deep in autumn and be heavily manured. Planting is usually done early in March. Pieces of the thick roots 4 in. to 6 in. long, called ' thongs ' by gardeners, are cut from the old root-stalks in March, and are planted 12 in. apart in rows 1½ to 2 ft. apart. This operation may be performed annually ; but if plants are to remain for a few years in the same place, it will be necessary to give more space so as to permit the free use of the hoe or fork between the rows, and also to afford more air and light. Instead of raising plants from cuttings of the roots in this way, seeds may also be sown in drills 1½ to 2 ft. apart, afterwards thinning the seedlings out so as to leave about a foot between each plant. In autumn, when the large grey-green wavy leaves have decayed, it may be advisable to cover the crowns with a little heap of ashes or sand, or litter.

Blanching.—This operation consists in excluding the light from the young shoots when they commence to grow in spring.

A box, large pot, hand-light, or even a heap of leaves placed over each crown will serve the purpose in the open air, but ashes or sand over the crowns should be removed first. When the shoots are long enough, a little light may be given just to give a tinge of colour to the tips. Where one has a warm greenhouse or moist hot-bed, the roots may be lifted from December to February, and placed in the warmth and in the dark. In this way blanched shoots can be secured very early in the season.

Market-gardeners in England commence forcing Sea-kale from the end of October till the end of February. The best and earliest crowns are first selected and planted side by side in beds 4 to 5 ft. across, and heated underneath by hot-water pipes. The roots are embedded in the soil to the tops, and after planting receive a good drenching with water to settle the soil round them. They are afterwards covered with clean strawy litter to a depth of 12 or 18 in., and in severe weather mats are placed overhead on cross-bars. From fourteen to twenty-one days—according to the time of year—are required to produce the leaf-stalks. The litter is then taken off, and all the crowns that are ready are taken from the bed, and prepared for market. As soon as one set of crowns is finished, others are ready to take their place, and thus a constant supply is kept up till the plants forced in the open air begin to yield.

French growers plant the Seakale roots in beds the same width as the frames generally in use for forcing Carrots, Radishes, Lettuces, etc. The beds are thus 4 ft. 5 in. wide, and have an alley or path-way between them. Five furrows about 4 in. deep are drawn, and the plants are placed in them at the end of March or early in April, the two outer rows being about 7 or 8 in. from the margin. This allows about twenty-five " crowns " to each light. After planting, the crowns are freely watered when necessary, and the soil which had been drawn up in little ridges when making the furrows or drills is gradually washed down, and eventually covers the crowns. Towards the end of June or early in July the waterings cease, as the plants will be then established and well furnished with their large wavy grey-green leaves.

About the end of October or early in November, the dead and dying leaves are removed, and the beds are cleaned up and hoed lightly, preparatory to having the frames placed over them. The pathways are also dug out 10 or 12 in. deep, some of the soil being placed in the frames for " earthing up " the Seakale crowns, the remainder being placed close at hand for filling the trenches after the forcing is finished.

When the temperature in the frames falls to 60° Fahr., the trenches between the frames are filled with good manure. Each crown is covered with a heap of soil about 6 to 7 in. deep, and the entire portion to be forced is covered with dry leaves or straw to hasten vegetation. About a month afterwards the first shoots may be cut, taking care to sever each one about half an inch above the " collar " of the plant. A second crop may be secured from the same plants by covering the crowns again, and treating in the same way. After the second forcing the crowns are of little use, and should be destroyed. The frames and old manure are then removed, and the pathways are filled up again with soil.

Another method of forcing Seakale is to lift the plants in October or November, and place them side by side on a manure bed giving a heat of 60° to 65° Fahr., which has been covered with about 6 in. of mould before the frames are placed on it. About sixty-four crowns are thus forced under each light, and the frames are " lined " with manure in the way described above, to secure a steady temperature. The plants are given a gentle watering after some nice rich sandy mould has been worked in between them, and also over them to a depth of 2 or 3 in. A covering with straw, leaves, or litter completes the work, and shoots may be cut at the end of eighteen or twenty days.

Seakale may also be forced in warm cellars at the same period. The crowns are lifted, cleaned, and planted on a few inches of rich mould, and are afterwards covered 2 or 3 in. deep with the same compost. More or less water is necessary, according to the dryness or humidity of the atmosphere, and at the end of three or four weeks shoots will be ready for cutting.

SPINACH

The Spinach (*Spinacia oleracea*) is an annual plant, native of Persia, whence it was introduced to Spain in the middle of the sixteenth century by the Arabs. According as to whether the seeds (really the " fruits ") are " prickly " or " smooth," two distinct kinds of Spinach are recognised, each with several varieties— all highly valued for their soft bright green leaves.

At one time French gardeners used to grow Spinach on hot-beds, on which young plants were pricked out about 4 in. apart in November, so as to be ready for gathering from December to March. This system of forced cultivation is, however, no longer adopted or rarely practised. I have, however, seen young plants lifted from the open ground in February or early in March. All the leaves were cut off, and the plants thus mutilated were placed in frames between Gotte Lettuces that were nearing maturity on the top of

Early Carrots. Spinach grown in this way branches out a good deal, and produces fine foliage in about three weeks after planting. The entire plant is pulled up when ready, and is fit for sale when the roots have been cut off. It realises a much higher price than open-air Spinach at the same period.

About the middle of August seeds of the variety known as " Monstrous Viroflay " may be sown on nicely prepared, but not deeply dug, soil, either in drills, 9 to 12 in. apart and about 2 in. deep, or " broad-cast " at the rate of about 1 lb. of seed to 160 square yards—or a little over 5 poles or " rods " of ground. After sowing, the soil should be trodden down firmly and raked over. To hasten germination, a good watering may be given, especially if the soil is inclined to be dry, or the seeds may have been soaked in water three or four times before sowing. Under favourable conditions Spinach leaves may be picked from this first sowing about the end of September, taking care that only the largest leaves at the bottom are picked first, and by hand.

Another sowing of Spinach may be made in October for gathering in spring, using the varieties known as " Flanders " or " Prickly Long Standing " on this occasion.

Some growers sow Spinach in December amongst Carrots in frames, picking the leaves with care when ready.

About the middle of February Spinach may be sown at intervals of two or three weeks, until the end of July. The early sowings should be made on warm sunny borders, while the later ones in summer are best on north borders, or between rows of other vegetables which will shade them from strong sun-shine.

If the plants show signs of running to seed during the summer months, they are best destroyed, and replaced with other crops.

The chief care with Spinach is to give the plants plenty of water, either morning or evening, during dry weather.

TURNIPS

Turnips (*Brassica napus*) are now grown as a forced or " primeur " crop on hot-beds more than formerly. Early in January a bed is made up to give a tem-perature about 70° to 80° Fahr. The surface is then covered with a layer, about 7 or 8 in. thick, of rich mould, made up of two parts of old manure and one part of rich loamy soil passed through a sieve.

The seeds are usually sown neither broad-cast nor in drills, but in small holes made in the compost with the finger. About every 6 in. a hole 1 in. deep is made with the finger, and into each one or two Turnip seeds are dropped—making about eighty to one hundred to every light.

The surface is then levelled with a piece of wood and lightly watered, after which mats are spread over the lights until germination has taken place—generally in four or five days.

As soon as the first leaves after the seed-leaves have developed, the young Turnips must be thinned out, so that only one plant is left in each little hole. About a month or six weeks after sowing, that is, about the middle of February, the lights are taken away to place over a second sowing of Turnips. The first crop must then be protected during the night with mats thrown over the frames. If, however, the weather at this period is very severe, it is safer to leave the lights some time longer until all danger is over.

To ensure active growth in the frames, the young Turnips should be watered frequently—almost every day—and at the same time abundance of air must be given on all favourable occasions by tilting up the lights on the leeward side.

In about seven or eight weeks after sowing the seeds, and treating as above described, the young Turnips are fit to pull.

About the middle of February another sowing of Turnips may be made on a somewhat cooler bed than the first crop, and in the same way. If the weather is favourable, the lights from the first crop may now be taken off,

FIG. 56.—" MARTEAU "
OR HALF-LONG WHITE
VERTU TURNIP.

and placed over the second just sown. These lights in turn are taken off the second crop in due course and placed over the third sowing of Turnips.

A fourth sowing of Turnips may be made about the middle of April on the bed from which the second crop has been gathered, the same set of lights being used for protection successively. It will be noted that only two different beds are used for the four crops. When these are cleared, the beds may be utilised for the culture of Melons.

Making holes with the finger is rather a primitive

method, and has been discarded by some growers. These have a frame made exactly the size of each light. As many cross-pieces as there are to be rows of Turnips are fixed to these frames, and in each cross-piece as many pegs are fixed as there are to be Turnips in a row. All that is necessary is to press the frame with the pegs downwards upon the pre-

FIG. 57.—HALF-LONG WHITE FORCING TURNIP.

pared soil, and each peg makes a hole in which the Turnip seeds are then sown.

The variety of Turnip favoured by the Parisian grower is called "*Marteau*" or "Half-long Vertu" (fig. 56), owing to its quick growth and excellent quality. It is the variety *par excellence* for the first early crops, and Parisian gardeners have made thousands of pounds by its cultivation. The "Half-long White Forcing" Turnip (fig. 57) is also an early variety well suited for frame culture. "Red Flat

Milan " and " White Flat Milan " are suitable either
for early crops under lights or for later crops in the
open air.

One of the most popular Turnips for market is the
" Long Vertu " or " Pointed Croissy," of which
large quantities are sold in the Paris markets during
the summer months.   Indeed, it was the only variety
I saw in the market in August.

PART III

CALENDAR OF OPERATIONS FOR THE YEAR

UNDER ordinary circumstances it would be more convenient to commence a calendar of operations in January. With intensive methods of cultivation, however, it is somewhat different. The month of August is generally recognised as the beginning of the cultural year for the intensive cultivator, hence it is, therefore, more convenient to begin the calendar in this volume at that period.

Under each month in the year—from August in one year to July in the following—the principal operations, as detailed in the preceding pages, have been noted briefly, merely as reminders to the grower what ought to be done in each month. It is important that seeds should be sown, pricked out, or transplanted at the proper time, otherwise the crops may mature too late to be of any particular value, especially to the commercial grower. Although Paris is somewhat farther south than London by about 3 degrees, there is really very little difference in the climatic conditions. As temperature, however, is an all-important point in gardening, and especially when conducted

205

on intensive principles, it has occurred to me that it might be useful to the grower to have some idea of the average temperature of the air and the soil for each month of the year. I have, accordingly, extracted this information from Lindley's *Theory and Practice of Horticulture*, the figures given being those taken for ten consecutive years in the Royal Horticultural Society's late Gardens at Chiswick some years ago. The mean air temperatures at Paris have also been included for the purpose of comparison. It will, of course, be remembered that places farther north or south than London will have different mean temperatures, and it would be well for growers to find them out and place them in a conspicuous place in their gardens for future reference. So far as the rainfall is concerned, there is very little difference between that of Paris and London—the average rainfall in the former being about 23 in., and 25 in. in the latter. Here again, of course, great variation is to be found, as more rain generally falls on the western side of Great Britain than on the eastern.

By the kindness and courtesy of the authorities at the Observatory Department of the National Physical Laboratory at Kew, I am enabled to give below the meteorological averages of Rainfall, Sunshine, and Temperature which have been extracted from the records by permission of the Meteorological Council. These figures may serve for comparison with observations made in other parts of the kingdom.

From these figures it will be seen that the popular expression " February fill dyke " is by no means accurate, as February and March are generally the driest months in the year. At Ealing the average rainfall for forty years has been 25·39 in., although in 1908 there was as much as 27·34 in. And during the past three years, 1906, 1907, 1908, there have been 248, 240, and 242 dry days respectively.

METEOROLOGICAL AVERAGES AT THE KEW
OBSERVATORY

	RAINFALL. Average in inches for 35 years, 1871-1905.	SUNSHINE. Average in hours for 25 years, 1881-1905.	TEMPERATURE. Average for 35 years, 1871-1905.
January ..	1·788	41·3	38°.9 F.
February ..	1·541	55·0	39°.9
March	1·533	104·7	42°.1
April	1·625	147·4	46°.9
May	1·711	199·1	52°.3
June	2·184	195·0	58°.8
July	2·442	207·9	62°.4
August	2·255	188·6	61°.2
September ..	2·145	141·1	56°.7
October ..	2·734	92·3	49°.0
November ..	2·203	49·5	43°.7
December ..	1·926	35·9	39°.6
Yearly Means and Total ..	24·087 in.	1457·9 hrs.	49°.3 F.

AUGUST

Mean temperature of Soil at 1 ft. deep, 61°.80. Air, 61°.28 (Paris 65°).

Cabbages.—Seeds of " Ox Heart " may be sown on old hot-beds or on borders for succession.

Carrots.—A small sowing of " Early Paris Forcing " may be made on old beds, or on warm borders for winter use.

Cauliflowers.—Sow seeds of " Lenormand " and " Early Erfurt," afterwards pricking seedlings out under lights. Cauliflowers nearing maturity should be kept growing freely by copious waterings and frequent use of the hoe. Keep a watch on caterpillars.

Corn Salad.—Sow early in the month ; afterwards at intervals of three or four weeks till the end of October for succession crops if necessary.

Endives.—Those planted out at end of June should now be ready for tying up. They require plenty of water during hot weather. The " Green Batavian " Endive should now be planted out.

Lettuces.—Cos and Cabbage varieties sown in July should be ready for planting under cloches about the end of the month—one Cos lettuce and three Cabbage Lettuces under each cloche.

The " Passion " and " Black Gotte " varieties of Cabbage Lettuces should now be sown for early supplies. The seedlings should be pricked out under lights or cloches when ready.

Spinach.—Winter Spinach should be sown in the open borders early in the month.

Turnips.—Seed should be sown to yield nice roots in October and November.

Hot-beds.—Manure for these should be prepared and turned over, and old Melon beds should be cleaned up.

SEPTEMBER

Mean temperature of Soil at 1 *ft. deep,* 57°.54. *Air,* 56°.14
(Paris 60°).

Cauliflowers.—Sow seeds of " Dwarf Early Erfurt " about the middle of the month, and prick out seedlings in other beds in October when large enough. The plants from these must be wintered in frames, and will be ready for planting amongst Carrots in March next.

Leeks sown in May, and transplanted in July, will be ready during this month.

Lettuces.—The Cos or Romaine varieties are sown under cloches and will be ready for pricking out in early October.

Cabbages.—Another sowing may be made of " Ox Heart."

Corn Salad, Turnips, Carrots, and **Radishes** may also be sown—the last named on warm sheltered borders.

Onions sown in August will be ready for pricking out preparatory to the final planting in October.

Endives.—Seeds of " Ruffec " and " Green Batavian " may be sown to be pricked out under cloches in October.

OCTOBER

Mean temperature of the Soil at 1 ft. deep, 51°.52. Air, 49°.35 (Paris 48°).

Lettuces.—The small kinds, if sown early in the month, will be ready for cutting about February. " Passion " Lettuces sown this month may be pricked out and grown on under cloches or in frames till January, and then planted out.

Lettuces sown in August will be ready for planting early this month, if not at end of September, on raised sloping beds under cloches.

About the middle of the month, Lettuces (Cos and Cabbage varieties) may be sown for early forced crops. The kinds for this sowing should be " Black Gotte," " Passion," and " Blonde Paresseuse."

14

Cabbages, " Ox Heart."—Seedlings will now be ready early in October for pricking out, so as to be ready for planting on warm sheltered borders by the middle of November.

Endives planted out in open-air beds in July will be ready this month. Plants from the September sowing should be pricked out under cloches.

Corn Salad may be sown in the open air.

Asparagus.—Crowns two or three years old should be taken up before the frost, and placed on hot-beds for forcing (see p. 76).

Radishes may be sown on warm sheltered borders early in the month. In the event of frost it would be well to cover with lights or protect with straw or litter.

NOVEMBER

Mean temperature of the Soil at 1 *ft. deep* 46°.01. *Air,* 42°.89 *(Paris* 44°).

Lettuces, " Small Black Gotte."—The young plants from seeds sown in August will be ready for planting on hot-beds by the middle of this month. Others will be ready for pricking out under cloches.

Cabbages.—About the middle of the month young plants of " Ox Heart " sown in August will be ready for planting out 18 in. apart on warm borders, having been already pricked out of seed-beds early in October.

Cauliflowers grown under cloches or lights should be protected with mats at night in case of frost.

Celery should be protected against frost with litter or bracken.

Carrots—" Grelot " or " Early Forcing Horn "—may

be sown about the end of the month on hot-beds, and amongst them thirty or thirty-six **Cabbage Lettuces** (" Black Gotte ") may be planted under each light.

Radishes are often sown in these lights after planting the Lettuces. They grow quickly and are gathered before they interfere with either the Lettuces or the Cabbages.

Spinach should be sown about the middle of the month under lights. The " Flanders " variety will resist the cold well.

Ventilation.—The cloches and lights under which " Passion " Lettuces are grown must be ventilated as freely as possible to prevent the leaves decaying.

DECEMBER

Mean temperature of Soil at 1 *ft. deep,* 41°.13. *Air,* 38°.14
(*Paris* 41°).

Lettuces.—At end of month the beds which have carried " Black Gotte " Lettuces are turned over, and some fresh manure is added previous to making up for another crop.

The ground for " Passion " Lettuces in the open should be deeply dug, and after levelling and raking may be covered with a layer of old manure. The Lettuces should be planted about the end of January.

Cabbages.—Seedlings that have not been pricked out will be left in beds until February, but should be protected against hard frosts with a little straw, litter, or bracken when necessary.

Carrots may be sown on all hot-beds in which Cos Lettuces or Cabbage Lettuces are to be planted.

Cloches.—At this season one Cos Lettuce (*grise*

maraîchère) and three Cabbage Lettuces ("Black Gotte") may be grown under each glass on the hot-beds.

Radishes may also be thinly sown just after planting the Lettuces.

Manure.—The old manure which is to be used for covering the beds next season should be got into ridges about 3 ft. high and 10 ft. apart, and fresh manure may be wheeled in between them for the formation of the beds.

JANUARY

Mean temperature of the Soil at 1 ft. deep, 40°.07. Air, 38°.21 (Paris 41°).

Asparagus.—Seeds may be sown on hot-beds about the middle of the month. Crowns two or three years old may be forced in the way described at p. 76.

Cabbages.—Any young plants that have been frosted should be covered with straw or litter to prevent quick thawing, which often does great harm to the plants.

Carrots.—Sow "Early Forcing Horn" with Radishes on beds that are to be planted with Lettuces.

Cauliflowers.—Seeds of "Lenormand" or "Second Early Paris" may be sown to produce plants for putting between the Cos Lettuces later on.

Cucumbers.—Sow seeds about the end of the month.

Lettuces.—The white-leaved "Passion" raised from seeds sown in October should be ready for planting in the open air in mild weather about the end of the month, or sooner, to be ready in April or May. Before planting, seeds of "French Breakfast Radishes" may be sown on the same soil. " Black Gottes " may be planted on the top of beds in which Radishes and Carrots are sown.

Any Lettuces attacked with mildew should be removed and burned. Clean healthy plants should fill the vacant places and have a little flowers of sulphur strewed round them.

Melons.—Seeds of the " Cantaloup " varieties should be sown about the end of the month, to have fruits in May and June.

Radishes.—Seeds of " French Breakfast " kinds and " Early Forcing Horn " Carrots may be sown in beds on which " Gotte " Lettuces are to be planted.

Spinach.—An early supply may be obtained by sowing on hot-beds during the month.

Tomatoes.—Seeds may be sown to produce plants for putting under cloches in May.

Protection.—Frames and cloches must be protected from frost with mats at night, and fresh manure must be added if necessary to keep up the temperature.

FEBRUARY

Mean temperature of the Soil at 1 ft. deep, 39°.74. Air, 38°.42 (Paris 38°).

Lettuces.—Look over the plants in frames and remove old or decaying leaves regularly. Others may be planted under cloches—one Cos Lettuce in the centre of three Cabbage Lettuces. The bed holds nine rows (see p. 162).

Melons.—Seeds of " *Cantaloup Prescott fond blanc* " may be sown again. When large enough transfer each seedling to a 3-in. pot in nice rich loam.

14 *

Endives.—Sow the "Rouen" variety about the middle of the month on a hot-bed, afterwards pricking out the little plants in another bed, and eventually transferring to cold frames or cloches when ready early in April. "Paris Green Curled" (or La Parisienne) is another good variety for sowing at this season.

Cauliflowers.—About middle of month make a sowing on hot-bed to have young plants to put under cloches in March.

Cabbages.—Seeds may be sown on hot-beds in the latter half of the month to produce plants in succession to those sown in August or September. Plants from the autumn sowing should be planted out after the middle of the month.

Turnips.—Sow early in the month on old Lettuce beds that have been re-made. The half-long or "*Marteau*" variety is recommended at this season by French growers, but "Early Snowball" or other English varieties would probably yield excellent results.

Radishes.—Sow again on beds carrying Lettuces or Carrots. Sow also in the open air in warm sheltered spots.

Spinach.—Sow at intervals of two or three weeks from the middle of the month in the open air.

Celery and Celeriac.—Sow seeds at end of month or early in March.

Mats.—In January, February, and March, when the mats are taken off the lights or cloches in the morning, they should be stood on edge and spread out against walls and fences to drain and dry if they have been soaked with rain during the night.

MARCH

*Mean temperature of Soil at 1 ft. deep, 40°.96.   Air, 40°.49
(Paris 42°).*

Lettuces.—Cos varieties may be planted in the hot-beds. In beds sown with Radishes, Lettuces, and Carrots in January, the Radishes will have been all gathered by this time, leaving only the Lettuces and Carrots. " Passion "• Lettuces in frames must be well ventilated both day and night.

Melons.—Young plants will be ready for planting in frames at end of this month, and should have the main shoot stopped beyond the second leaf as early as possible.

Cauliflowers.—Sow seeds of " Lenormand " for growing in old hot-beds in the open during the summer months. Cauliflowers from seeds raised about the middle of last September, and pricked out in October, should now be planted on the hot-beds containing Carrots. They may also be planted in beds with Cabbage Lettuces and Spinach or Radishes.

Protection.—Mats must be placed over cloches and frames at night when frost is anticipated. They should not be removed in morning until after the thaw has set in.

Cucumbers.—Seeds of long green varieties may be sown between the middle of March and middle of April, to be ready for final planting about the end of May.

Carrots.—The last sowing of " Half-long " varieties on hot-beds is made early this month, also under cloches, and in the open borders. Radishes may be sown at same time amongst those on hot-beds.

Leeks.—Sow in open air (see p. 141).

Spinach.—Sowings may be made between other crops such as Lettuces (Cos and Cabbage), Endives, Cabbages, etc., or in separate beds.

Sorrel may be sown during the spring and summer to keep up a supply of leaves.

Cabbages.—Sow for summer and autumn crops in the open air, and hoe between the Ox-Heart varieties in the open air.

Onions.—Early in the month seedlings that were not disturbed in the beds should be planted out.

Turnips.—The lights should be taken off these on all fine days and even at night if no frosts are feared. Mats should be handy for covering in case of sudden frosts.

Dandelions.—Seeds may be sown now and at intervals until June to produce plants for autumn and winter salads.

APRIL

Mean temperature of the Soil at 1 ft. deep, 46°.47. Air, 46°.57 (Paris 48°).

Cauliflowers.—After the first batch of Lettuces under cloches have been cleared, and the glasses have been moved over the other rows (as explained at p. 163), Cauliflowers may be planted in the places left vacant by the Cos Lettuces.

Cauliflowers from seeds sown in September may be planted in the open air about 2 to 2½ ft. apart (see p. 113).

Cabbages.—By the end of this month the " Ox

Heart" varieties sown last August will now be ready for cutting. Those sown in February will be ready for planting out about the middle of the month.

Lettuces.—The "Passion" variety, planted in January, will now be nearing maturity, and the space between each plant may be filled with a Cauliflower. The frames and lights may be taken away altogether from these crops, if necessary, about the end of the month, and used for a second crop of Melons.

Melons.—Those already in frames require careful ventilation each day when the weather is fine. Seeds should be sown each week to have plants ready later on for the beds as they become vacant.

Celery.—Make a sowing early in April, and prick out 3 in. apart in May on an old hot-bed. These are to follow Cauliflowers. Young Celery plants may now be placed in frames, from which Turnips, Radishes, and Carrots have been gathered.

Lettuces.—The Cos varieties grown on hot-beds will require attention. As the earlier plants are nearing maturity, the cloches covering them should be removed to cover the plants next in order of ripening, as explained at p. 163.

Carrots.—During this month attention must be given to weeding and thinning out, as the plants grow quickly. If necessary, the frames may be raised 2 or 3 in. by placing bricks or blocks of wood at corners, but manure should be previously banked up round frames to prevent soil from falling down afterwards.

Celeriac.—The young plants from seeds sown at end of February or early in March will be ready for pricking out on south borders or on an old hot-bed.

MAY

Mean temperature of Soil at 1 *ft. deep,* 53°.11.   *Air,* 53°.54
(*Paris* 58°).

Lettuces.—The last of the plants placed under cloches in February will be ready this month.   The first crop will be ready for pulling.

"Passion" Lettuces grown in cold frames or on warm borders will be ready for cutting.

Endives.—If the weather is mild and moist, Endives may be planted in the open ; and another sowing of " Rouen " may be made on a hot-bed.

Cauliflowers.—These may be planted on the edges of old beds that have borne a crop of Cos Lettuces. Cauliflowers in frames with Carrots must be ventilated both day and night, to harden them off.   They must be regularly watered.   Early in the month the frames and lights over these should be removed for Melons, if the weather is fine.

Tomatoes may be planted out under cloches this month (see p. 61).

Melons.—Prepare trenches 2 ft. wide and 1 ft. deep, and fill with two-thirds dry and one-third fresh manure for making Melon beds.   These are covered with soil from trench in next bed.   When Melons are planted, the lights are placed on frames and kept close and shaded for a few days (see p. 172).   Early in the month a final sowing of " *Cantaloup Prescott* " and " *Kroumir* " may be made.

Watering.—This is an important operation.   Abundance must be given to Melons well set in fruit, and also to Cauliflowers showing heads.

Leeks.—Make a sowing of " Long Winter Paris " to

be planted out in July in beds where Carrots and Cauliflowers have been grown. Water freely and hoe regularly.

Cornichons or **Prickly Cucumbers** may be sown on old hot-beds early in the month (see p. 129).

Celery.—Seeds of the " *Blond* " variety may be sown early in May for autumn use.

Radishes may still be sown in vacant places on beds or in the open air.

Endives.—About the third week in May sowings of the fine-leaved and broad-leaved varieties may be sown in the open, afterwards intercropping with Lettuces. Others maturing should be tied (see p. 139).

Celeriac.—The final planting should be done this month.

JUNE

Mean temperature of Soil at 1 *ft. deep,* 60°.02. *Air,* 60°.45
(Paris 64°).

Endives.—The " Rouen " variety should be planted out at end of month on old manure beds. Earlier crops will need tying up, and will be ready during the month.

The variety called " Ruffec " and " Green Batavian " may now be sown on old hot-beds to give a supply in autumn.

Carrots and **Cauliflowers** will be ready about the third or fourth week, and the beds on which they are grown may be used for Melons sown in May ; or the beds may be planted with **Endive** or **Celery**.

Each morning the Cauliflowers should be examined, and those developing heads rapidly should have some of the lower leaves detached and placed over them, to keep them pure white, otherwise they become browned and are not so valuable (see p. 114).

Cauliflowers and **Melons.**—A sowing of "Lenormand" Cauliflowers early in May will produce young plants that will be ready for planting among the Melons at the end of June—about four plants to each light.

Lettuces.—The last of the Cos Lettuces grown in frames or under cloches will now be disposed of.

Melons must be well watered this month, and have plenty of air, even at night-time in fine weather. Fruits from first crop will be ready by end of month.

Catch Crops.—The beds that have borne Carrots and Cauliflowers, and have been prepared for Endive or Celery, may have catch crops of Spinach or Breakfast Radishes sown on them after the Endive or Celery has been planted.

Cabbages.—About the middle of June seeds of Winter Cabbages and Savoys may be sown on old beds, the seedlings being ready for planting out at the end of July if they have been well watered and not sown too thickly.

JULY

Mean temperature of Soil at 1 ft. deep, 62°.85. Air, 63°.40 (Paris 67°).

Asparagus raised from seeds sown in January will be ready for planting out about the middle of July. The best plants only should be chosen.

Carrots, early, and **Spinach** may be sown as catch-crops on beds of other crops, and must be well watered, to be ready in October.

Endives sown in June may now be planted in the open-air beds, and will be ready by October. " Ruffec " and " Green Batavian " are the best at this period.

Cauliflowers may be planted in the Endive beds, one between every two.

Celery.—When the Cauliflowers that were planted in the Carrot beds in March have been cleared, their place may be taken by the Celery plants raised in March.

Melons must now be watched regularly for the ripening of the fruits, and lights may be removed altogether if weather is fine.

Lettuces.—Cos and Cabbage varieties may be sown in open beds for planting at the end of August.

Manure.—During this month stable manure must be obtained in large quantities and stacked into heaps (see p. 19).

PLAN OF A FRENCH GARDEN

Although no two gardens devoted to intensive cultivation are exactly alike in shape, size, or system of cropping, the diagram overleaf may serve to give a fairly good idea as to the lines upon which a French garden is generally laid down. In actual practice various modifications would naturally be made according to the site and aspect; and entrances and exits would appear at the most convenient spots in the fences or hedges.

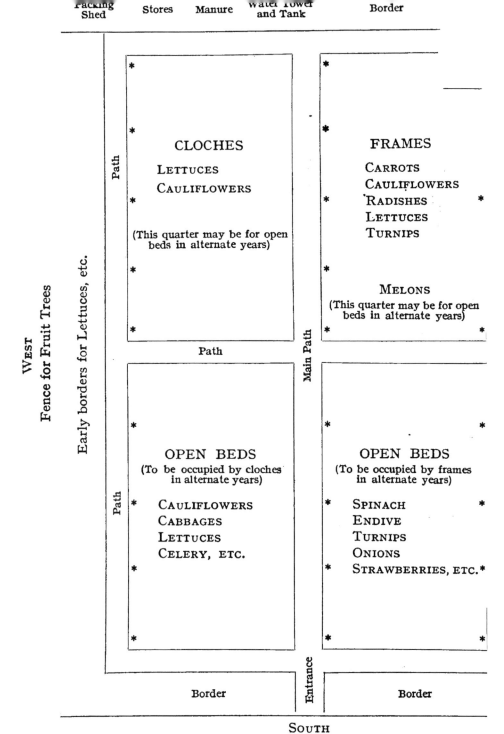

PLACKING
SHED STORES MANURE WATER TOWER BORDER
                       and Tank

WEST
Fence for Fruit Trees

Early borders for Lettuces, etc.

Path

CLOCHES

LETTUCES
CAULIFLOWERS

(This quarter may be for open
beds in alternate years)

Path

FRAMES

CARROTS
CAULIFLOWERS
RADISHES
LETTUCES
TURNIPS

MELONS

(This quarter may be for open
beds in alternate years)

Main Path

OPEN BEDS

(To be occupied by cloches
in alternate years)

CAULIFLOWERS
CABBAGES
LETTUCES
CELERY, ETC.

OPEN BEDS

(To be occupied by frames
in alternate years)

SPINACH
ENDIVE
TURNIPS
ONIONS
STRAWBERRIES, ETC.

Border

Entrance

Border

SOUTH

PLAN OF A FRENCH GARDEN

* = Standpipes for watering (see p. 49).

INDEX

Rhubarb, 63
Rotation of crops, 55
Rumex Acetosa, 193
   montanus, 193

Salesmen, commission, 29
Salsafy, 192
Scaroles, 134
Scolecotrichum melophthorum, 177
Scorzonera, 192
Seakale, 195
Seedlings, pricking out, 52
   transplanting, 53
Seed sowing, 49
September, work for, 208
Shading, 53
Site for a French garden, 7
Slugs, 167
Soil and its treatment, 10
Solanum Melongena, 131
Sorrel, 193
   Maiden, 193
Spawn, Mushroom, 183
Spinach, 199
Spores, Mushrooms from, 185
Standpipes, 49
Strawberries, 60
Sulphate of copper solution, 89, 166

Sunshine averages, 207

Taraxacum Dens-Leonis, 130
Temperature averages, 207
Tephritis Onopordinis, 120
Thatcham, garden at, 3
Thermometers, 45
Thinning out seedlings, 51
Thrips, 178
Tilts for cloches, 41
   for frames, 40
Tomatoes, 61
Tragopogon porrifolius, 192
Transplanting seedlings, 53
Turnips, 201

Valerianella olitoria, 123
Vegetable market, Paris, 57
   Marrows, 62
   Oyster, 192
Ventilation, 53
Violets, 63

Water, distribution of, 16
Watering, 47
   in winter, 48
Waterpots, 45
Water supply, 13
Windmills, 14
Wireworms, 166
Witloof, 122

Printed by Hazell, Watson & Viney, Ld., London and Aylesbury.

Chas. Toope (F.R.H.S.) & Son,

Stepney Square, High St., Stepney,

LONDON, E.

TELEPHONE: E.3497.   TELEGRAMS: "TOOPES, LONDON."

MANUFACTURERS AND PATENTEES OF

Heating Apparatus for Greenhouses, Conservatories, Motor Houses, Kennels,

etc.

FOR
GAS,
OIL,
OR
COKE
HEAT-
ING.

Send for fully Illustrated

Catalogue, Free.

The Best by Test.

State size of
Greenhouse,
temperature
required,
and we will
be pleased to
send esti-
mate free.

☞ *The only Reliable Heaters in the U.K.* ☜

Toope's Perfect Propagator.

Hot Air or Hot Water, from **14/-**
complete.

Toope's
" Little Vixen "
Garden Frame Heaters.

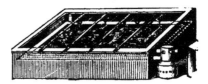

For Oil, Gas, or Coke.   For
French Intensive Culture.

——— ALSO ———

French Bell Glasses, Mats, French Frames, etc.

SYRINGES, SPRAYERS, HOSE, GARDEN TOOLS, MOWERS, etc.

The very best Material only used.   Prices to suit all.   Superior Goods.
Quick Deliveries.

*Send for separate Catalogues of Coal and Coke Heaters, also Incubators
and Poultry Appliances.*

WORKS ON AGRICULTURE AND GARDENING

WORKS BY WILLIAM ROBINSON

THE ENGLISH FLOWER GARDEN AND HOME GROUNDS

DESIGN AND ARRANGEMENT SHOWN BY EXISTING EX-
AMPLES OF GARDENS IN GREAT BRITAIN AND IRELAND,
FOLLOWED BY A DESCRIPTION OF THE PLANTS, SHRUBS
AND TREES FROM THE OPEN-AIR GARDEN, AND THEIR
CULTURE.

Illustrated with many Engravings on Wood.   Tenth Edition.
Medium 8vo.   15s. net.

THE VEGETABLE GARDEN

ILLUSTRATIONS, DESCRIPTIONS AND CULTURE OF THE
GARDEN VEGETABLES OF COLD AND TEMPERATE
CLIMATES.

BY MM. VILMORIN-ANDRIEUX,
of Paris.

English Edition published under the direction of W. ROBINSON.

Numerous Illustrations.   Demy 8vo.   15s. net.

"'The Vegetable Garden' is a complete and authoritative work upon all that concerns
vegetables, and stands unique among works on the subject. It should be on the bookshelf
of everyone interested in vegetables, for it is not a work for the grower alone."—*Garden.*

CHEAPER EDITION.

THE WILD GARDEN

OR, THE NATURALIZATION AND NATURAL GROUPING
OF HARDY EXOTIC PLANTS, WITH A CHAPTER ON THE
GARDENS OF BRITISH WILD FLOWERS.

Illustrated by Alfred Parsons.   Demy 8vo.   10s. 6d. net.

THE GARDEN BEAUTIFUL

HOME WOODS AND HOME LANDSCAPES.

Illustrated with Engravings on Wood.   Demy 8vo.   **7s. 6d.** net.

ALPINE FLOWERS FOR GARDENS

ROCK, WALL, MARSH PLANTS AND MOUNTAIN SHRUBS.

Third Edition Revised.   With Illustrations.   8vo.   **10s. 6d.** net.

GOD'S ACRE BEAUTIFUL;

OR, THE CEMETERIES OF THE FUTURE.

With 8 Illustrations.   8vo.   **7s. 6d.**

NATURE TEACHING

BASED UPON THE GENERAL PRINCIPLES OF AGRICULTURE, FOR THE USE OF SCHOOLS.

BY FRANCIS WATTS, B.Sc., F.I.C., F.C.S., and WILLIAM G. FREEMAN, B.Sc., A.R.C.S., F.L.S.

Crown 8vo.   **3s. 6d.**

SYNOPSIS OF CONTENTS.

THE SEED—THE ROOT—THE STEM—THE LEAF—THE SOIL—PLANT FOOD AND MANURES—FLOWERS AND FRUITS—WEEDS—ANIMAL PESTS OF PLANTS—GLOSSARY. *Appendices.*—I. SUGGESTED COURSES—II. APPARATUS AND MATERIALS REQUIRED —INDEX.

"Forms a welcome change from the many appearing under similar titles in that it is avowedly based upon experiments, and treats of things about which the writers really know and have not merely read up."—*Nature.*

ELEMENTS OF AGRICULTURE

A TEXT-BOOK PREPARED UNDER THE AUTHORITY OF THE ROYAL AGRICULTURAL SOCIETY OF ENGLAND.

BY W. FREAM, LL.D.

Seventh Edition.   With numerous Illustrations.
Crown 8vo.   **3s. 6d.**

CONTENTS.

SOIL—Origin and Properties of Soils—Composition and Classification of Soils— Sources of Loss and of Gain of Soils—Moisture in Soils—Improvements of Soils—Tillage —Implements for Working Soils—Manures and Manuring.

THE PLANT—Seeds and their Germination—Structure and Functions of Plants— Cultivated Plants—Weeds—Selections of Seeds—Implements for securing Crops—Grass Land and its Management—Farm Crops—Fungus Pests—Insect Pests.

THE ANIMAL—Structure and Functions of Farm Animals—Composition of the Animal Body—Foods and Feeding—The Art of Breeding—Horses, Cattle, Sheep, Pigs: Their Breeds, Feeding and Management—The Fattening of Cattle, Sheep and Pigs— Dairying—Index of Plants—General Index.

THE CULTURE OF FRUIT TREES IN POTS

BY JOSH BRACE.

With Illustrations.   Large Crown 8vo.   **5s.** net.

CONTENTS.

I.—INTRODUCTORY—Houses and their Construction—Selection of the Site—Pots—Soil—Stocks—Span-roofed Houses –Three-quarter Span—Lean-to Houses—Ventilation—Inexpensive Houses—Wire Houses—Protection against Birds—Water—Cost of Construction.

II.—THE FURNISHING OF THE HOUSE—Number of Trees Required—Arrangement of the Trees—Beds and Borders—The Need for Separate Compartments.

III.—CULTURAL DETAILS—The Forms of Trees –Potting—Soil—Potting-hook and Prong—Perforated Pots—Method of Forcing—Pruning—Pinching—Hide-bound Trees—Surface Dressing—Number of Fruits on a Tree—Cost of Trees—Longevity, etc.

IV.—VARIETIES OF FRUITS—Peaches and Nectarines—Apricots—Plums—Cherries—Apples and Pears– Baking Pears—The Mulberry—The Fig—The Vine.

V.—INSECT AND OTHER PESTS—Green Fly—Brown Aphis—Red Spider—Thrip—Earwigs—Weevils—Ants—Mildew, etc.

VI.—A CALENDAR OF OPERATIONS IN THE UNHEATED HOUSE FOR EACH MONTH OF THE YEAR.

VII.—MISCELLANEOUS OBSERVATIONS—Flavour—Gathering the Fruit—Fruit Trees for Decorative Purposes—Miscellaneous Directions, etc.

EXPLANATORY NOTES TO PLANS—INDEX.

" A valuable contribution to a very interesting phase of fruit-culture."—*Field.*

" Brief, clear, and well-founded in the practical wisdom born of life-long experience in the kind of gardening it describes, the work cannot but be serviceable."—*Scotsman.*

A HANDY
BOOK OF HORTICULTURE

AN INTRODUCTION TO THE THEORY AND PRACTICE OF GARDENING.

BY F. C. HAYES, M.A.,

Rector of Raheny ; Lecturer in Practical Horticulture in
Alexandra College, Dublin.

With Illustrations.   Crown 8vo.   **2s. 6d.** net.

CONTENTS.

PART I.—GENERAL PRINCIPLES—Principles and Practice of Gardening—The Soil: its Nature and Preparation—The Food of Plants: Manuring—Half-hardy Plants and Greenhouse Culture—Hot-beds and Cold Frames—The Gardeners Natural Enemies—Seeds and their Treatment—Budding, Grafting, Inarching, Layering, and Striking.

PART II.—DEPARTMENTS—The Spring Garden—Summer and Autumn Flowers—Herbaceous and Rock Border combined—Alpine Borders—Roses—Ferns: their Nature and Classes—Construction of Ferneries—Climbers—Lawn Shrubs—Shrubs and Autumn Tints—Treatment of Lawns—Culture of Vegetables—Growing Fruit and Pruning Trees.

PART III—TYPES OF HARDY FLOWERS—Heartsease, Violas, and Violets—Scillas and Gentians—Irises—Lilies—Anemones—Carnations — Chrysanthemums — Cyclamens and Tuberous Begonias—Christmas Roses—Wallflowers (Cheiranthus)—Primroses—Annuals, Biennials, and Perennials — Fragrant Plants—Cordyline Australis — Water-lilies (Nymphæa)

PART IV.—KALENDAR FOR MONTHS—Gardening in January—Gardening in February—Gardening in March—Gardening in April—Gardening in May—Gardening in June—Gardening in July—Gardening in August—Gardening in September—Gardening in October—Gardening in November and December—A Short List of Reference Books on Gardening for Students—Specimen Examination Papers—Index.

" Not so big that it need frighten the ardent amateur, nor so much of a primer that it may be disdained by the fairly accomplished gardener, it has a good scheme. The first part, consisting of eight chapters of general principles, in simple, non-technical language, is a model of useful information in a small space ; the second part deals with departments of gardening the third, with types of flowers, and the fourth is a calendar to work by "
—*Daily Chronicle.*

THE SOIL

AN INTRODUCTION TO THE SCIENTIFIC STUDY OF THE
GROWTH OF CROPS.

BY A. D. HALL, M.A. (Oxon.),

President of the Rothamsted Station (Lawes Agricultural Trust);
First President of the South-Eastern Agricultural College.

With Diagrams. 5s. net.

The science of agriculture has advanced considerably since the first edition of this book was published, so Mr. Hall has taken advantage of the need for a reprint to produce what is practically a new book. A good deal of fresh material has been added, the latest statistics have been included and the whole text has been thoroughly overhauled and re-set, bringing everything completely up to date.

"An excellent and up-to-date text-book. . . . The complete knowledge of the soil and the part it plays in the nutrition of the plants requires investigation along three lines, which may be roughly classed as—chemical, physical or mechanical, and biological. It is exactly these with which the author deals, and although it is in no sense an exhaustive treatise, a general outline has been given of all the recent investigations which have opened up so many soil problems, and thrown new light on difficulties that are experienced in practice."—*Gardeners' Chronicle.*

THE BOOK OF THE
ROTHAMSTED EXPERIMENTS

BY A. D. HALL, M.A. (Oxon.),

President of the Rothamsted Experimental Station; First President of the
South-Eastern Agricultural College.

ISSUED WITH THE AUTHORITY OF THE LAWES AGRICULTURAL TRUST COMMITTEE.

With Illustrations. Medium 8vo. 10s. 6d. net.

CONTENTS.

FERTILISERS AND MANURES

BY A. D. HALL, M.A. (Oxon.),

Director of the Rothamsted Station (Lawes Agricultural Trust) ;
Author of " The Soil," " The Book of the Rothamsted Experiments,"
etc.

Crown 8vo.

This book, which is a companion volume to the same Author's book on
" The Soil," deals not only with the history, origin, and nature of the various
fertilisers and manures in use in this country, but also with their effect upon
the yield and quality of crops in practice.   Much unpublished material has
been drawn from the Rothamsted experiments, but other series of field
experiments have also been utilised to furnish examples elucidating the
principles upon which manuring should be based.   As befits a book intended
for the practical man as well as the student of agricultural science, a good
deal of attention is given to the making, value, and utilisation of farmyard
manure, while another important chapter deals with the manuring of each of
the staple crops of the farm, according to the character of the rotation in
which it finds a place.

A HISTORY OF GARDENING
IN ENGLAND

BY THE HON. MRS. EVELYN CECIL.

With Illustrations.   Medium 8vo.

ON THE MAKING OF GARDENS

BY SIR GEORGE SITWELL.

Square Demy 8vo.

This is an attempt to analyse the " garden magic " of Italy and to lay
down new principles of design.   The Author is probably better acquainted
than any other living Englishman or Italian with the old gardens of Italy:
he attaches much importance to the psychological side of the problem, and
deals with the philosophy of beauty in a way which will appeal to every
lover of a garden.

LONDON : JOHN MURRAY, ALBEMARLE STREET, W.

MR. MURRAY'S
LIST OF BOOKS

ON

HORTICULTURE,
AGRICULTURE

AND

COUNTRY LORE.

LONDON : JOHN MURRAY
50A, ALBEMARLE STREET, W.1

LB

INDEX

Books on Horticulture, Agriculture and Country Lore.

TREES AND SHRUBS HARDY IN THE BRITISH ISLES. By W. J. BEAN, Assistant Curator, Royal Botanic Gardens, Kew. " Here is a book which stands out by itself as the work of a master of the subject. No one who cares for trees and shrubs can possibly do without it . . . . a mass of knowledge and experience which is unrivalled." Mr. H. J. ELWES, in Country Life. With over 250 Line Drawings and 64 Half-tone Illustrations. Two Volumes. Second Edition. 48s. net.

CONIFERS AND THEIR CHARACTERISTICS. By CHARLES COLTMAN-ROGERS. This book is an invaluable aid for students and others in identifying the many different species of trees included in the category of the Natural Order of the Coniferæ, and it also gives in anecdotal form much reliable and interesting information on their life-history.

HARDY ORNAMENTAL FLOWERING TREES AND SHRUBS. By A. D. WEBSTER. Author of " Practical Forestry," etc. " We commend the book on its undoubted merits as a reference work and guide." Journal of Horticulture. Third Edition. 5s. net.

COMMERCIAL FORESTRY IN BRITAIN : ITS DECLINE AND REVIVAL. By E. P. STEBBING, Head of the Department of Forestry, University of Edinburgh. The need for a national scheme of afforestation ; what it will do for the country ; the necessity for the use of public funds, and the methods by which the State can obtain the best return for its outlay, are discussed in this book by one who is an acknowledged authority on the subject. With Frontispiece. 6s. net.

BRITISH FORESTRY : ITS PRESENT POSITION AND OUTLOOK AFTER THE WAR. By E. P. STEBBING. " Mr. Stebbing writes with authority. He puts the case extremely well, and he puts it with moderation." The Field. Illustrated. 6s. net.

THE BULB BOOK,

or, Bulbous and Tuberous Plants for the Open Air, Stove, and Greenhouse.   By JOHN WEATHERS.   Containing particulars as to descriptions, culture, propagation, etc., of plants from all parts of the world having bulbs, corms, tubers or rhizomes (orchids excluded).   "Meritorious, remarkable, informative and accurate, almost beyond criticism ; the most complete bulb book of the present day, and likely to remain a classic."   Journal of Horticulture.   Illustrated.   18s. net.

THE SMALL GARDEN BEAUTIFUL.

By A. C. CURTIS.   "Mr. Curtis is both an idealist and a practical gardener giving a lucid explanation of eminently practical methods."   Westminster Gazette.   Third Edition.
Illustrated.   5s. net.

ITALIAN GARDENS OF THE RENAISSANCE.

By JULIA CARTWRIGHT (Mrs. Ady).   "The studies before us are full of charm, and breathe the very spirit of that spring-time of the modern world when Europe awoke again to the loveliness of Nature."   The Outlook.   Illustrated. 12s. net.

THE GENUS ROSA.

By ELLEN WILLMOTT. Drawings by Alfred Parsons, A.R.A. With 128 Coloured Plates and 56 Drawings of Fruits in Black and White.   "The outcome of many years of observation, labour and study, this magnificent folio must take a higher place than any existing monograph of the Rose."   The Garden. In 25 Parts.   21s. net each.

A HANDY BOOK OF HORTICULTURE.

An Introduction to the Theory and Practice of Gardening. By F. C. HAYES, M.A., Lecturer in Practical Horticulture in Alexandra College, Dublin.   "Not so big that it need frighten the ardent amateur, nor so much of a primer that it may be disdained by the fairly accomplished gardener, it has a good scheme."   Daily Chronicle.   Illustrated.   5s. net.

IN A COLLEGE GARDEN.

By VISCOUNTESS WOLSELEY, Citizen and Gardener of London.   "A serious contribution to an important problem [Gardening for Women] as well as being, for the general reader, a book of the pleasant garden, a book to refresh all those who have ever cast a seed and waited for the flower."   Saturday Review.   Illustrated.   6s. net.

THE CULTURE OF FRUIT TREES IN POTS.

By JOSH BRACE. The result of very many years' practical experience of this popular form of cultivation. "A valuable contribution to a very interesting phase of fruit-culture." The Field. With Illustrations. Second Impression. 6s. net.

FRENCH MARKET GARDENING : With Practical

Details of Intensive Cultivation for English Growers. By JOHN WEATHERS. With an Introduction by WILLIAM ROBINSON. "This useful and interesting work deals with every phrase of that form of intensive culture known as French Gardening. It is well written and is easily understood. Fruit, Flower and Vegetable Trades' Journal. Illustrated. 4s. 6d. net.

THE KITCHEN GARDEN AND THE COOK.

An Alphabetical Guide to the Cultivation of Vegetables, with Recipes for Cooking them. By CECILIA MARIA PEARSE "The most extensive ever published in regard to the cookin of vegetables." Aberdeen Daily Journal. 4s. 6d. ne

TOWN GARDENING.

A Hand-book of Trees, Shrubs, and Plants, suitable for Town Culture in the Outdoor Garden, Window Garden, and Greenhouse. By B. C. RAVENSCROFT. This work, the result of the author's experience as a practical gardener in London and suburbs, may be fully relied upon. Second Edition. Revised and Enlarged. 4s. 6d. net.

A HISTORY OF GARDENING IN ENGLAND.

By The Hon. Mrs. EVELYN CECIL (ALICIA AMHERST). "It is so well-written that reading it is a pleasure. No one can read it intelligently and fail to obtain a good idea of what gardening in this country has been and is."—The Field. Third and Enlarged Edition. Illustrated. 15s. net.

THE BOOK OF FLOWERS.

By KATHARINE TYNAN and FRANCIS MAITLAND. This book makes no pretence at all to completeness or scientific knowledge. It is as though one walked in a garden or the fields and picked at random a flower here and a flower there, tying them loosely into a bunch. 6s. net.

THE SMALL FARM AND ITS MANAGEMENT.

By JAMES LONG, Member of the Small Holdings Committee. Second Edition, thoroughly revised throughout and brought up to date.

HINTS TO FARM PUPILS.

By E. WALFORD LLOYD. An indispensable book for those starting to learn farming and anxious to pick up all the information they can with a view to getting quickly into the business. A PRACTICAL FARMER writes: " In a general way it is very good, nor have I read anything so concise or with so much real sound stuff in it before." 2s. 6d. net.

COMMON WEEDS OF THE FARM AND GARDEN : Including the Weeds of Chief Importance, both

of Arable and Grass Land, and Weed Seeds. By HAROLD C. LONG, B.Sc. (Edin.), of the Board of Agriculture and Fisheries, in collaboration with JOHN PERCIVAL, M.A., F.L.S., Director of the Department of Horticulture and Agriculture, University College, Reading. With 98 Illustrations.
6s. net.

ELEMENTS OF AGRICULTURE.

By W. FREAM, LL.D. A Text-book prepared under the authority of the Royal Agricultural Society of England. Edited by J. R. Ainsworth-Davis, M.A., Principal of the Royal Agricultural College, Cirencester. Tenth Edition. Illustrated.
7s. 6d. net.

PRACTICAL AGRICULTURAL CHEMISTRY.

By S. J. M. AULD, D.Sc., Ph.D., F.I.C., F.C.S., and D. R. EDWARDES-KER, B.A., B.Sc. This book is intended as a practical handbook in Agricultural Chemistry, for students working through courses of instructions for the London B.Sc. Degree in Agriculture, and other examinations of a similar type and standard. Illustrated. 6s. net.

THE CHEMISTRY OF THE GARDEN :

A Course of Practical Work for Teachers and Students of Horticulture, Gardening and Rural Science. By D. R. EDWARDES-KER, B.A. (Oxon.), B.Sc. (Lond.). Contents : The Chemistry of Plants—The Chemistry of Soils—The Chemistry of Manures and Fertilisers—The Chemistry of Sprays and Washes—Appendix. 2s. net.

By Sir A. D. HALL, K.C.B., F.R.S.,

Formerly Director of the Rothamsted Experimental Station.

THE SOIL.

An Introduction to the Scientific Study of the Growth of Crops. A new edition of this standard work, thoroughly revised throughout, and re-set. " A remarkably well-arranged, well-written volume. In its way it is a masterpiece." The Times. Third Edition. Illustrated. 7s. 6d. net.

FERTILISERS AND MANURES.

" He is able to give innumerable practical notes on the results of experiments in manuring, and it is these which we think will form the chief attraction to the cultivator, as the results of actual work on the land do not always coincide with theories based on laboratory work alone ; a great work for Agriculture, and for Horticulture also." Horticultural Advertiser. Eighth Impression. Illustrated. 7s. 6d. net.

THE FEEDING OF CROPS AND STOCK.

An Introduction to the Science of the Nutrition of Plants and Animals. " The products of Sir Daniel Hall's knowledge and experience are always welcome in the manuals which come from his facile pen, but that now under notice is expecially so, as it is complementary to his works on Soils and Manures." Agricultural Economist. 4th Impression. Illustrated. 6s. net.

AGRICULTURE AFTER THE WAR.

" Small in size, but great in value, the work deserves wide circulation and careful consideration." The Times. Third Impression. 5s. net.

A PILGRIMAGE OF BRITISH FARMING.

"A marvellously accurate and illuminating account of agriculture. It must be for some time one of the most valuable books in the library of English agricultural literature."— Home Counties, in the Daily Chronicle. Second Impression. 7s. 6d. net.

THE BOOK OF THE ROTHAMSTED EXPERIMENTS. Second Edition Revised by E. J. RUSSELL,

D.Sc., F.R.S. Director of the Rothamsted Experimental Station. Issued with the Authority of the Lawes Agricultural Trust Committee. This new edition has been brought up to date, and new chapters are added, discussing work carried out during the past ten years. 12s. net.

SHOOTING DAYS.

By Captain ERIC PARKER, Shooting Editor, " The Field."
" He fondles the memory of each satisfactory shot, recalls
every stone and bush, and brings the scent of bog-myrtle, or
the gurgle of the trout-stream, or the tap-tap of beaters'
sticks, or the thrill of an oncoming covey, before the reader
with amazing vividness. His book will be a treasury of real
delight not only to every exiled and homesick sportsman, but
to everyone who has known the free joys of moor, field, and
stream." The Spectator. Second Impression. 7s. 6d. net.

LETTERS TO A SALMON FISHER'S SONS.

By A. H. CHAYTOR. " We are glad to welcome a new
edition of one of the best practical books on salmon fishing that
has ever been written." The Field. Second Edition.
Illustrated. 12s. net.

THE WILD SPORTS AND NATURAL HISTORY OF THE HIGHLANDS.

By CHARLES ST. JOHN. With the Author's Notes and a
Memoir by the Rev. M. G. Watkins. Illustrated. Ninth
Impression. 6s. net.

FISHING AND SHOOTING.

By SYDNEY BUXTON. With Illustrations by Archibald
Thorburn. " He writes in so lucid and charming a manner,
that we have not often read a book on fishing with greater
interest." The Field. Second Edition. 12s. net.

PARTRIDGE DRIVING.

By CHARLES E. A. ALINGTON. Some practical hints on
increasing and preserving a stock of birds and on bringing
them over the guns. With Diagrams. 6s. net.

DOG BREAKING.

By General W. N. HUTCHINSON. The most expeditious,
certain and easy method. With odds and ends for those who
love the dog and gun. Popular Edition. Illustrated.
7s. 6d. net.

By WILLIAM ROBINSON.

THE ENGLISH FLOWER GARDEN

AND HOME GROUNDS. Design and Arrangement followed by a Description of the Plants, Shrubs and Trees for the Open-air Garden and their Culture. Illustrated with many engravings on wood. Twelfth Edition. 15s. net.

THE VEGETABLE GARDEN.

Illustrations, Descriptions and Culture of the Garden Vegetables of Cold and Temperate Climates. By MM. VILMORIN-ANDRIEUX. English Edition published under the direction of WILLIAM ROBINSON. Second Edition with an Addendum by W. P. Thomson. Illustrated. 25s. net.

THE WILD GARDEN, or, THE NATURALISATION AND NATURAL GROUPING OF HARDY EXOTIC PLANTS. With a Chapter on the Garden of British Wild Flowers. Bound in Vellum. Fifth Edition. Illustrated. 12s. net.

ALPINE FLOWERS FOR GARDENS.

Rock, Wall, Marsh Plants, and Mountain Shrubs. Fourth Edition. Illustrated. 10s. 6d. net.

THE GARDEN BEAUTIFUL.

Home Woods and Home Landscapes. Illustrated with Engravings on Wood. 7s. 6d. net.

THE VIRGIN'S BOWER.

Clematis: Climbing Kinds and their Culture at Gravetye Manor. Illustrated. 3s. 6d. net.

GRAVETYE MANOR ; or, TWENTY YEARS' WORK ROUND AN OLD MANOR HOUSE. Being an Abstract from the Tree and Garden Book of Gravetye Manor, Sussex, kept by the Owner. Folio. Illustrated. Bound in Vellum. £3 3s. od. net; Paper, £2 12s. 6d. net.

GOD'S ACRE BEAUTIFUL ; or, THE CEMETERIES OF THE FUTURE. Illustrated. 6s. net.

BOOKS ON COUNTRY LORE.

THE HERON OF CASTLE CREEK : AN
OTHER SKETCHES OF BIRD LIFE.   By A. W. REE
Author of " Ianto the Fisherman," etc.   With a Memoir of t
Author, by J. K. Hudson.   Mr. Rees' previous volumes
Nature Studies won him a place which was all his own in t
great succession of writers who have made nature their them
This book consists of a series of studies of Bird Life, and als
chapters on Bird Watching and Animal Life in Winter.   Wit
Portrait.   7s. 6d. ne

CREATURES OF THE NIGHT.
A book of Wild Life in Western Britain.   By A. W. REE
" No one with a love of wild creatures can resist the charm
such a work, every page of which shows knowledge, insigh
and sympathy ; a fascinating work."—Daily Telegraph.   Illu
trated.   7s. 6d. ne

A COTSWOLD VILLAGE.
By J. ARTHUR GIBBS.   With a Portrait of the author an
other Illustrations.   " It is a delightful work."   Pall Ma
Gazette.   " It has been a real pleasure to read it."   Th
Guardian.   Ninth Impression. 6s. ne

WILD LIFE AT THE LAND'S END.
By J. C. TREGARTHEN.   Records and Observations of th
Habits and Haunts of the Fox, Badger, Otter, Seal, etc., an
of their Pursuers in Cornwall.   " We should say that his boo
has all the charm of the best conversation, of a sportsma
of the old school, mingled with that of a gamekeeper and
poacher, men who knew the night as well as they knew th
day, a man as well as a fox."—Daily Chronicle.   Illustrate
                                                          12s. ne

THE LIFE STORY OF AN OTTER.
By J. C. TREGARTHEN.   " The book is one in whic
naturalists will especially rejoice, because they will find wha
cannot be found elsewhere ; but there is no class of reade
above the age of twelve who would not find satisfaction in thi
speaking description of Western scenery and graphic tale o
the most mysterious of its denizens."—Times. Illustrated
                                                          5s. net

THE GAMEKEEPER AT HOME ; or, SKETCHES OF NATURAL HISTORY AND RURAL LIFE.

By RICHARD JEFFERIES. " Delightful sketches. The lover of the country can hardly fail to be fascinated wherever he may happen to open the pages. It is a book to read and keep for reference, and should be on the shelves of every country gentleman's library."—Saturday Review. Illustrated. 6s. net.

THE AMATEUR POACHER.

By RICHARD JEFFERIES. " We have rarely met with a book in which so much that is entertaining is combined with matter of real practical worth."—Graphic. 6s. net.

SPRING IN A SHROPSHIRE ABBEY.

By Lady C. MILNES GASKELL. "A beautifully illustrated book, half garden book and the rambling thoughts of a cultivated woman, half fiction and Shropshire folklore."— Evening Standard. Illustrated. 10s. 6d. net.

FRIENDS ROUND THE WREKIN.

By Lady C. MILNES GASKELL. A further collection of history and legend, garden lore and character study, such as was gathered up in the former volume, " Spring in a Shropshire Abbey." Illustrated. 10s. 6d. net

FIELD PATHS AND GREEN LANES IN SURREY AND SUSSEX.

By LOUIS J. JENNINGS. This book will be found interesting, and in some degree useful, to those who find an unfailing source of pleasure in wandering over England, deeming nothing unworthy of notice, whether it be an ancient church or homestead, a grand old tree, a wild flower under a hedge, or a stray rustic by the roadside. It is a genuine account of personal experiences recorded, as a rule, on the very day they occurred: Fifth Edition. Illustrated. 6s. net.

WS - #0038 - 300522 - C0 - 229/152/15 - PB - 9781334277535 - Gloss Lamination